WITH GOD on the HIKING TRAIL

Nathan Chapman

HARVEST HOUSE PUBLISHERS
Eugene, Oregon 97402

Cover by PAZ Design Group, Salem, Oregon

WITH GOD ON THE HIKING TRAIL
Copyright © 2002 by Nathan Chapman
Published by Harvest House Publishers
Eugene, Oregon 97402

ISBN 0-7369-0706-8

Printed in the United States of America.

02   03   04   05   06   07   08   / BP-CF /   10   9   8   7   6   5   4   3   2   1

*To my wife Stephanie,
my companion on the trail of life.*

Acknowledgment

I am forever grateful for the friendship I have with avid outdoorsman and writer Eric Kramer. Many of the insights I've gleaned came first from his heart and the experiences we've shared on the trail.

1

A Place to Start

*For since the creation of the world God's invisible
qualities—his eternal power and divine nature—have
been clearly seen, being understood from what has been
made, so that men are without excuse.*

Romans 1:20

I was introduced to the joys of hiking and back-packing by my dad, an enthusiastic outdoorsman and hunter whose books, songs, and paintings reflect his love for the great outdoors. The seed was planted when I asked him about an old, tan backpack hanging on the wall of our garage. This external frame pack had no logo or big, padded shoulder straps like the modern counter-parts. He told me that while stationed on an aircraft car-rier in the Navy, he used his free time to hike in France. I imagined this aged backpack resting on my father's shoulders during times of soul searching and peace on starry nights in the mountains of Europe. I began to dream of my own trips…perhaps portions of Dad's quiet serenity I have always admired awaited me in the wilder-ness.

While Dad seemed really excited to see me showing an interest in hitting the trail as soon as possible, I know now that he had a greater hope. He encouraged me to "go take a hike" because he knew that after a few trips, I would begin to see truths of God articulated in nature.

My father knew that spending time alone in God's creation could serve as a vital part of my reaching adulthood and intimacy with Jesus. And that's exactly what happened.

While trekking through the forests of this great nation, I've seen the amazing beauty of God's creation and experienced unforgettable moments with Him. With His handiwork as the backdrop, God revealed truths about His Word and illuminated life-altering aspects of walking with Him daily. I offer some of these timeless insights with a sincere hope that each day's reading will encourage you to spend time with God while on the trail or at home.

Whether you are a day hiker, weekend hiker, or a serious backpacker out for weeks at a time, we have a common bond—we revel in God's power and divine nature as revealed in His Creation. So, off we go! And like I always say at the beginning of a hiking expedition, "Don't think about the top of the mountain, that'll get you down. Just enjoy the next step!"

Lord Jesus, thank You for this time in Your creation. Help me always to look to You while witnessing the beauty You've created. Only You can heal and satisfy my soul. I praise Your holy name, amen.

2

The Little Blue Line

The words of a man's mouth are deep waters,
but the fountain of wisdom is a bubbling brook.
Proverbs 18:4

The beginning of the day's route followed a fast-moving, deep river. On the map, it was marked by a little blue line. Because so many rivers were on the map, my father, sister, and I ignored the instinct to fill our water bottles. So by the end of the day, we were thirsty as we turned left onto a side trail, finally nearing the end of our five-mile, uphill hike. We were a few miles from Clingman's Dome, the highest point in Tennessee, which I had never hiked before. The altitude of the ridges and the July heat began to wear on us. We hadn't seen water for miles, but there was still one more chance to find it. According to the map, a stream was just over the ridge where we planned to camp. That little blue line, which meant a creek was only a few hundred yards away, kept us moving along.

When we got to the location where a river should start, there were large-leafed plants and fallen, rotten trees. My legs weakened and my heart sank. Even the lowest point I could find offered only muddy patches and wet rocks. I was not only discouraged, I was also a little worried. By conserving water, we were able cook dinner, but we had an arid hike for a few miles the next morning. Thankfully we finally found a water source.

As I realized how much I had counted on human knowledge, I thought of the many times I'd trusted in the wisdom of the people around me. I remembered that this broken world is filled to the brim with "new thoughts" and advice marked by "blue lines" that assure us that safety and nourishment are waiting just over the ridge. This can be a deadly deception.

God's Word says, "If any of you lacks wisdom, he should ask God, who gives generously to all without finding fault" (James 1:5). God is ready to lead us! His wisdom is bountiful and accessible. When we request wisdom from Him, He will not lead us to a muddy basin on a hillside. God promises that His guidance and loving care are readily available, and He invites us to drink from His "bubbling brook."

Thank You, God, for making Your wisdom accessible to me all the time. I need Your guidance and heavenly leading. Please keep me from following the worldly wisdom that keeps me away from You. I ask, right now, for Your wisdom. Amen.

3

Trailblazers

The way of the sluggard is blocked with thorns,
but the path of the upright is a highway.
Proverbs 15:19

Eric Kramer and I rounded a turn on the Appalachian Trail (AT), struggling to take each step through the knee-deep snowdrifts. We were blinded by the high winds that carried freezing rain and more snow. We heard a voice yell "Ho!" and wondered who else was crazy enough to hike in such unkind and unforgiving weather.

We learned that his trail-name was Chip. Yelling to be heard, we discussed the weather and found a bond in our suffering. At the end of our conversation, the stranger said he had forged a path through the deep snow, which would help us stay on the trail. My first thought was, *Yeah, like you know any more than us!*

Although skepticism was my first reaction, Eric and I were so exhausted, cold, and frustrated that we had no option but to rely on Chip's footprints in order to conserve energy and make it to the shelter. Sure enough, we found the shelter just to the left of where his boots had trod.

Later that evening, the other rugged souls who joined us in the drafty and exposed shelter for the night told us that Chip was a trail legend. He had hiked the entire 2,200-mile AT 13 times! We were regaled with stories of how Chip could follow a snow-covered trail for miles without markers or signs along the path. He knew the trail that well!

As I listened to the tales, I thought of today's verse. I wondered why the path of the upright is referred to as a "highway." Why were the way of the sluggard and the way of the upright so different? Then it hit me—the sluggard is constantly trying to blaze a new trail!

On a highway, many people have gone before us in the same journey. Any thorns on the path have already been trampled until they no longer grew. If Eric and I had ignored Chip's advice, we might have made wrong choices concerning which way to go. By following his advice, our hike was much easier because Chip had trampled through the higher drifts that slow a hiker down.

Chip was able to provide a temporary trail and an easier hike because he had been there before. And in this same way, when we study the Scriptures and learn from older saints in our congregations, we don't have to blaze new trails. As wise Christians, we can listen to and watch people who have been down the trails of life, even when their paths were covered with snow and difficult to traverse. From them we can avoid many of the pitfalls this world offers.

I am grateful to my ancestors in the faith for staying on the trail. I need their footprints and offer them to those who come after me.

Jesus, thank You for guiding the saints who have gone before me on the paths of righteousness. Help me follow and make the trail easier for those who come after me. In Your name I pray, amen.

4

Take It Like a Hiker

Blessed are you when people insult you, persecute you and falsely say all kinds of evil against you because of me.

Matthew 5:11

Do you remember your first extensive hiking trip? Mine was one of the most physically challenging experiences I've ever had. I consulted very few people, and I planned big. My maiden route would take me from my freshman college dorm to a camping area in the Cherokee National Forest. My target campsite was 25 miles away, and I planned to walk to it on Saturday and return on Sunday—a 50-miler for my first trip. (In retrospect, this doesn't sound like an activity of someone *enrolled in* an institution for higher education; it sounds like the activity of someone *in* an institution!)

Though I don't know how, I did finish that first hike. The severe pain lasted for three days. Oddly enough, the physical pain wasn't the worst. The hardest part of the trip was the unexpected yelling and obnoxious jeers that I received along the way from not-so-nice people in their cars. I hadn't figured out that we hikers can look strange and awkward, especially when we use walking sticks. I endured comments such as, "Where's your mountain, ski boy!" and "Get a car, hippie!"

I didn't yell back or raise a fist. Instead, I reminded myself that I was walking 50 miles while they were riding in their cars. I imagined how hard it must be for them to understand why a person would trade the comforts of a kitchen and a warm bedroom for a campfire and an old tent. Their drive-by insults didn't stop me—they added to the adventure because my goal was sure. I was trekking and creating a memory that would last a lifetime.

Much like hikers, Christians can look ridiculous sometimes. We smile at those who persecute us, give money away without telling others, and share the good news of Jesus. To people who have chosen lifestyles that focus on personal comfort and convenience, we must really look strange. Nonbelievers don't understand how giving freely of our time and money helps us gain eternal things. They can't see where the path ends—the arms of our heavenly Father!

The persecutions we receive can encourage us. If we choose, those jeers and cries can blend with the sounds of our boots pounding the pavement and become signs that we are moving forward in our spiritual walk. We are on our way to the great reward Jesus promises. Keep on trekking!

Right now, Lord, I forgive anyone in my past who has persecuted me in any way. Thank You for the journey, even though the insults of others sometimes makes it feel harder than it really is. Give me strength to find the journey's end. In Your name I pray, amen.

5

Last-Minute Planning

Suppose one of you wants to build a tower. Will he
not first sit down and estimate the cost to see
if he has enough money to complete it?

Luke 14:28

The Smoky Mountains, with their intense beauty, carefully protected wildlife, and well-maintained trails, are a great place to experience nature, but there are strict rules and regulations. One of these is that a backcountry hiker must register the plans for the hike and make reservations for many of the shelters he or she would like to stay in. Each night must be accounted for, and sometimes a trip must be altered because a shelter is booked up. Planning early is the key.

I didn't know this valuable information the first time I went to the Smokies. I was shocked to find that the wild had been tamed so much that reservations were necessary! I discovered this when I was getting my gear ready on that first afternoon. A park ranger came up and asked me whether I had registered my trip. I responded, "Huh?" I was informed that if I failed to register my trip I could count on him finding me later, fining me $200, and making me exit the forest! He curtly pointed to a pay phone and a large sign that listed the number and office hours of the ranger station. I sheepishly walked over, dialed the number, and filed my trip plans.

When the ranger asked me about my plans a few minutes later, I showed him that the first day I had charted a 3-mile hike. The second day's hike was 16 miles. The third day I was going to backtrack the 16 miles and return to civilization. The park official immediately informed me that 16 miles was more than I could handle. Having never hiked in the Smokies, I figured he was underestimating my abilities. I could run 3 miles in 22 minutes. Even if each mile took twice as long, 16 miles was not going to be a problem.

After 2 miles of hiking, I realized that the 16 awaiting me the next day were going to cause more pain than I wanted to imagine. I turned around, walked to the phone, and changed my reservation. The 8 miles I planned seemed more reasonable. I started my trip again 2 hours late, already feeling in my muscles the difficult hiking I had done. I was frustrated because my poor planning slowed me down and made my trip much harder. As I hiked to the first camp, I thought of other times I had failed to investigate the details and costs of an activity.

I thought of how often I want to look beyond the planning stage because my focus is on being "out there," moving forward, and tallying the miles behind me. But Jesus says, "Wait, count the costs, make sure you know what it means to follow Me."

Jesus knew that our hearts can deceive us. He knew that as much as we want to follow Him, sometimes the journey can be harder than it looks. He wants us to avoid the ridicule that comes with not being able to finish what we've started. That's why He encourages us to plan ahead.

As we move forward in our life journey, it's important to remember that stopping and thinking about what we are doing is a good thing because it prepares us for what's ahead. Maybe God is calling you to the ministry. If so, take a few days to plan, seek God, and count the losses and gains related to that decision. If God is calling you back to school, or to have children, or to change jobs, make sure you know that He has equipped you for the task.

Thank You, Lord Jesus, for helping me plan ahead. Please give me the patience to stop and think about my journey with You and the rewards of being in Your presence. In Your name I pray, amen.

6

David's Shield

*You are my hiding place; you will protect me from trouble
and surround me with the songs of deliverance.*

Psalm 32:7

Sometimes in the wee hours of the morning, I wake up and frantically feel around in my tent for my flashlight. "What's that sound?" I say to myself. "I know that crunch means big trouble." Being in the woods at night oftentimes ignites my imagination and I overreact. My mind conjures up the worst—I might see a shadow with two ears and gigantic paws on the tent or hear the serpentine sound of a warning rattle.

On one particular trip, however, the danger was very real. The last morning of my hike brought me to within 30 yards of a mother bear and her cub—and mother bears are known for ferociously protecting their young. Because of the smell of the food in my pack, I knew I had a big problem. They were lumbering directly at me with a smooth, purposeful gait. I stood up and walked backward for about 100 yards. I watched intently to make sure the beasts didn't follow. I glanced all around me making sure that another cub was not nearby, knowing that if I stood between the mother and a little member of the family, things would get ugly. My heart pounded as I watched the two of them sniff and paw exactly where I had been sitting just moments before. I was completely alone and vulnerable to attack. After what seemed to be an eternity, the two bears wandered away.

After I made it home, I realized I had something in common with a famous warrior-king of Israel. King David, a champion against giants and beasts, was no stranger to this kind of situation. At least the animals I met weren't being aggressive like the lion and the bear David killed. A jealous king and a giant were not on my trail either. What was David's solution? What did he trust for protection from these adversaries? David knew the only true safeguard he could ever have was walking with God.

When the bears came my way, I began to seriously pray for wisdom and protection. They weren't pretty prayers with King James-like vernacular. I wanted to be safe; I didn't feel like being lunch that day. I am grateful to report that I made it back to my vehicle in one piece. No claw marks or teeth scars were on my body. The mom and her little one paused and looked my way long enough to make my heart nearly jump out of my windbreaker, but she thankfully meandered off. *Whew!*

When we face dangers either in the forest or on the street, our responses can be similar to King David's, who placed the outcome of the situation in the hands of his Maker. Although this may not come naturally, it is the only true way to find safe passage in this perilous journey we call "everyday living." We can walk in confidence today because no lion is too fierce and no giant too tall that we can't depend on God for our protection.

Thank You, Father, for Your care. You know that in this physical world I have little protection of my own, but You can keep me safe. Help me put my trust in You. In Your name I pray, amen.

7

One Step at a Time

*Trust in the LORD with all your heart and lean not
on your own understanding; in all your ways
acknowledge him, and he will make your paths straight.*

Proverbs 3:5,6

All hikers know that to reach the destination they have to keep moving. Based on this principle, I've seen slow hikers complete journeys of great distances through dogged determination. Most of the Appalachian Trail through-hikers, for example, are not fast—they simply hike. The next step is their concern, not the miles in the distance. (Stopping to rest and eat is essential, of course.)

This hiking mentality also benefits those who desire to walk with God. Waiting on Him to direct our path has not been easy, especially when we wonder what we're to do with our lives and what God is calling us to do.

If you're like me, hearing the great stories of saints who received callings and went on to do great exploits for God adds to your anxiousness to know His will. But my impatient longing to know His plans for me fiercely competes with my reluctance to start walking without knowing the full description of the journey. To hit the trail without all the facts is a risk I struggle to take. I remind myself that the heroes of the Bible were not given every detail of their lives to come. The age-old stories reveal that God's trekkers knew little more than the next step. Joseph didn't know he would become a respected leader of Egypt when he was imprisoned. Abraham and Isaac started up the mountain, and Abraham most likely believed he would return alone.

As we take the great hike to eternity, we don't know what will come our way. Our job is to keep walking with Jesus. When we are willing to be in motion, God will give us the directions we need. Even when we know our specific calling or vision, we still have to stand up and put one boot in front of the other.

Are you waiting for God to hand you a detailed map of your journey to come? Seek intimacy with Christ, and He will show you which way to go.

Lord, I want to walk with You. I'm depending on Your leading to know which direction to go. Thank You for actively participating in my life. In Your name, amen.

8

The Weight of It All

Godliness with contentment is great gain.

1 Timothy 6:6

I entered a shelter along the Appalachian Trail around 4:30 in the afternoon. I had just witnessed incredible overlooks and had enjoyed nature's beauty up close. But there was one problem—my pack was too heavy. My shoulders were aching, and my neck felt like I needed one of those thick, white, padded neck braces. I knew the problem, but I was too embarrassed to confess my folly to the other hikers who were settling in for the night.

I had packed way too much food. I had canned hot-dogs and applesauce and prunes and granola bars—and those were just the snacking selections! I dreaded lugging the heavy pack the next day, so I started giving away food. It seemed a little odd to the other hikers, but they accepted the victuals I had (unknowingly) been carrying for *them*. I'd never been such a cheerful giver!

By overpacking, I gained a valuable mountain-climbing lesson: Each hiking trip helps us streamline our gear. I had created a disadvantage for myself by carrying more than my necessary portion. This brought to mind today's verse. God blesses folks with material things because we live in a world that requires the exchange of goods for physical existence. But if I carry too much bartering power, my journey will suffer. Understanding my limitations has become the most efficient and least painful way to carry my pack. Some of us are stronger than others and are able to carry greater loads. A close friend of mine carries large bank accounts in his "life pack," and it doesn't seem to ever slow him down. However, for others of us, our loads are lighter because our heavenly Father knows the limits of what we are able to heft. Seeking to fill our packs and pockets is a grave mistake. By learning to trust God more fully, we know He will meet all our needs...so there's no need to over-pack!

Lord Jesus, take away the fear that accompanies giving things away. Remind me each day that my needs are met by Your hand, and Your hand alone. Help me to assess what I need to carry and what I can give to others. In Your name I pray, amen.

9

Hike Your Own Hike

A friend loves at all times,
and a brother is born for adversity.
Proverbs 17:17

Sy Bagwell and I scoped out a designated camping area in the Smoky Mountains along the Appalachian Trail. We spotted a flat area of ground next to a couple of tents. Introductions were exchanged with two hikers who were on their way to Maine. Early in our conversation, they expressed concern for one of their fellow hikers who was yet to reach the campsite. Faced with the difficult dichotomy between concern and "every hiker hikes his own hike," these two backpackers were anxiously waiting for their buddy to arrive at the shelter. They told me and my friend that the missing member of their group had gotten sick, and his illness had kept them up most of the previous night as they tried to keep dry in an intense rain. They had hiked with him most of the day, but he insisted they go on and try to get some rest. The two hikers kept checking the ridgeline during our conversation and throughout dinner. When their pal finally arrived, the tension dissipated as his friends helped him settle in.

These guys were there for one another. The two healthy hikers didn't take their friend's dignity away by carrying his pack. They offered him companionship and encouragement.

Knowing how to help people in need is sometimes difficult. When those around us are hurting and trying to press on toward the prize, we need to step back, assess the situation, and pray about our actions. We can err by trying to carry their loads *for* them instead of *with* them. As we reach out to others, may we remember that love helps others succeed.

Thank You, Lord, that I don't have to make this journey alone. Help me wisely lend a hand when it's needed. Thank You for being my faithful companion along the way. In Your name I pray, amen.

10
The Real Me in the Mountains

Search me, O God, and know my heart;
test me and know my anxious thoughts.
Psalm 139:23

For a long while, every time I entered the forest I thought I could become this fearless mountainman who always knew the perfect routes and best modes of protection. Early in my hiking career, I convinced myself that if a bear were to ever come my way, I would most definitely be able to protect myself with a knife or with the pointed end of my walking stick. I was convinced that I had all the basic skills I needed to survive in the wild. Boldly I believed that by coming to the mountains I would don a new me who was braver and stronger and wiser than the nervous Nathan who sometimes faltered in daily challenges. Then one day I came face to face with reality.

After a long day of hiking I settled into camp tired and hungry. I gathered material for a campfire, then tried for an embarrassing one-and-a-half hours to get a fire going. All I got was a few puffs of smoke. After being reduced to a meal of dry noodles that stuck in my throat and nearly choked me, I felt defeated and worthless. My "Jeremiah Johnson" view of myself was quickly losing air. That's when the truth hit me.

I had been coming to the trail to shape my experiences instead of allowing my experiences in the mountains to shape me. Here's my journal entry for that night:

> Like with my hiking stick—do I really think I can, just because I'm here, fight a bear with a stick? No way! I'm the same guy who gets afraid of neighborhood dogs while I'm running. But that's OK. If something happens between me and a bear, I'm gonna do the most afraid thing there is to do. Mountainman Nate is just a figment of my imagination—but I am here before God and myself. I'm here with my faults and my strengths and my weaknesses.

Pride would have us believe we are invincible. Knowing where our fears and worries lie can help us. In His infinite wisdom and mercy, God sometimes shows us our weaknesses and exposes our anxieties in order to keep us humble and smart...and alive. The willingness to turn away from life's dangers is not always from weakness or lack of boldness. Sometimes it's from humility. As Christians, we should be bold in the Lord and trust Him to tell us when to walk away.

Lord, I acknowledge my limitations. Thank You for the gift of humility. I look to You to make me strong and help me remember weaknesses may always be with me—but so are You! In Your name I pray, amen.

11

The Forever River

As the deer pants for streams of water,
so my soul pants for you, O God.

Psalm 42:1

My favorite hiking routes are usually next to streams and rivers. I enjoy the beauty of my surroundings, and I also find comfort in knowing my thirst can be quenched at any time, and if I am injured I can cleanse my wound quickly in the cool, clear water.

While traversing through remote valleys, I've been able to experience the "Ansel Adams live" mountain stream landscapes that would make any of his black-and-white photographs turn green with envy. Memories of oil paintings that captured incredible stream scenes crack and peel as I take in the sight of the real thing. Kaleido-scopes of colors and sounds that dance and roar from watching a waterfall's choreography designed by the Maker Himself literally take my breath away.

Water is the liquid foundation of the creation process (see Genesis 1:2). It is absolutely necessary for our sur-vival. The psalmist uses the picture of a deer parched with thirst and longing for a stream of water to show us our search for God isn't merely an "eye-pleasing" scene. It is a longing for life.

The next time you're hiking by a stream, acknowledge your longing for God. Revel in the mystery and beauty

He created. He is our life when we partake of Him. As Jesus said, "If anyone is thirsty, let him come to me and drink" (John 7:37).

Lord Jesus, I'm awed by the incredible beauty of Your creation. Thank You for water's ability to quench our thirsts, and help me remember to look to You for that same quality. Let me drink deeply of the wisdom of Your Word and the soothing power of Your grace. I long to walk by Your side. In Your name, amen.

12
Out of His Way

God cannot be tempted by evil, nor does he tempt anyone;
but each one is tempted when, by his own evil desire,
he is dragged away and enticed.

James 1:14

If you've ever spent the night along a major trail, you've probably camped with elite backpackers who have chosen to dedicate their entire summer to hiking. On the Appalachian Trail, the enthusiasts are called "through-hikers." They're easy to spot because of the qualities that are the sure signs they are on their way from Georgia to Maine. First of all, they smell. They really stink. *Wheeoo!* Second, they are dedicated, driven people who seldom waver in their pursuit of a goal. And last, but not least, they talk about food *all* the time!

The standard staple for a through-hiker meal is usually some kind of rice or noodle because these meals are cheap and easy to cook. After a month on the trail, a big, juicy steak on a grill causes crazed looks and the whipping out of $20 bills! One particularly funny story came from a through-hiker who recalled the craving he had for a Subway sandwich. He said for three days all he could think about was getting his hands around one of those giant delights! He saw on his map that the AT crossed a road that led to a small town a few miles off the trail. He thought to himself, *Six miles. That ain't that far!* So he started walking. He hoped that a passerby would give him a ride, but no one came along. His craving led him a grueling total of 12 miles out of his way; he spent an entire day getting a sandwich!

In a similar fashion, desire can take over and lead us off God's trail if we're not careful. Whether it is a wayward physical desire or an ungodly craving for money, the journey into sin starts as a craving. In today's verse, James is very clear in saying that if we ponder desires in our minds that are against what God wants, sin is the end result. The food-crazed through-hiker is a great reminder that sin does not happen by accident—there are usually many steps that offer the opportunity to turn back to God.

Lord, right now I give You my thoughts. I confess my sin and declare my desire to be pure before You. Thank You for Your mercy and forgiveness, Lord Jesus. In Your name I pray, amen.

The Master Trail-Blazer

Keep my commands and you will live; guard my teachings
as the apple of your eye. Bind them on your fingers;
write them on the tablet of your heart.

Proverbs 7:3,4

My sister and brother-in-law helped my dad create a hiking trail on the family property. This trail takes only 30 minutes to hike and has great spots to picnic and enjoy the great outdoors. When I asked them what was included in the trail-making process, I was very surprised by their answer.

I learned that in order to make a good trail they had to find the safest route and the most convenient way around the fallen trees and large thornbushes. After several walk-throughs, they marked the route and went to work. It was back-breaking labor. They dug, chopped, and tilled the ground with shovels, hoes, and picks. They removed large stones and logs. And when the work was finished, they complained of sore backs and aching muscles. But their hard work paid off! When I hiked the trail, my feet moved easily across a smooth indentation on the forest floor. The violent upheaval they created resulted in a peaceful path through a serene forest.

Trailblazing is not so different from what God did on the stone tablets on Mt. Sinai. As he chiseled wisdom into the tablets, He was creating a path for His people—and all of humanity—to follow. Today's proverb encourages us to write God's commands on our hearts. As we follow God's ways, we become more Christlike. This process isn't always gentle.

Sometimes painful situations cut deep into our lives, but they are simply the tools used to keep us on God's path. When life deals us a blow, many times it's because our stony hearts need chiseling.

Jesus, soften my heart so that I'm more willing to grow in You. Keep me open to what You want to say to me. Help my heart of stone become a path of peace for others to follow. This I ask in Your name, amen.

14

Running into Perseverance

*If anyone would come after me, he must deny himself
and take up his cross daily and follow me.*

Luke 9:23

If you find yourself panting and wailing and whining your way up a steep incline on a trail, you probably say the same thing I say: "When I get back to civilization, I'm going to run more to stay in better shape! This pain will not happen next time!" Unfortunately, good intentions usually go the way of New Year's resolutions—disappearing into a deep ravine. They are gone. And the next steep mountain that looks doable on a map may turn out to be another looming tower of torture.

We know it is good to exercise daily, but it's so hard to set aside the time. Those of us who do manage to get the ol' heartrate up a few times a week have to make sacrifices to do so. Some folks jog in the mornings, others do aerobics in the evenings, and some of us watch others wheeze down neighborhood streets. The problem is that we usually don't have to be in great shape to do our daily tasks, but we're going to need that conditioning when we get to the mountains.

Daily conditioning is also important for Christians. Although we might go through an ordinary day without running into difficult temptations or faith-testing trials, we never know when hard times are on their way. Life's ups and downs require that we "work out" and strengthen our faith on a daily basis.

Today's Scripture deals with the daily activity of a Christian. When we "deny" ourselves, we are moving our focus away from us. When we exercise, we leave our normal tasks to make ourselves available for physical growth. It is the same with our Christian journey. If we are not separating ourselves from the world on a daily basis for conditioning and strengthening in Christ, then when the trail leads us out of the valley, we might find our ability to keep the pace compromised.

The next time you consider skipping your physical training, think about the mountains. And the next time you are going to skip your spiritual training, remember that life isn't always a gentle path in a valley.

Lord, sometimes hiking life's trail is difficult. Give me the self-control to prepare as best I can for those times. I know You'll give me the strength I need to make it through. You alone can provide that. Be with me in the valleys and on the mountains. In Jesus' name I pray, amen.

15

The Purifier

Create in me a pure heart, O God.

Psalm 51:10

Have you ever felt like you were holding someone's fate in your hands? Have you been tempted to walk away from that person without helping? One morning in a hiking shelter in the Smoky Mountains I faced this very thing.

Three guys from Colorado had lumbered into the shelter full of hikers the night before. Though they were a little noisy and disorganized, they finally settled in. The next morning they were very cordial and extremely apologetic for the disturbance. They explained that they had come from Colorado to share the local hiking trails. I was very impressed with their adventuresome spirit.

As I continued to visit with them, they revealed that they had missed some important planning details for this trip. They had made a long voyage from Colorado to the Tennessee wilderness. With all the necessary planning, they had forgotten a few things, including a way to purify their water for their week of backpacking. I could tell they were beginning to feel desperate. Knowing that I was leaving the Smokies that day, they asked if they could borrow my water purifier for the next week. Even though they promised to send it to me when their trek was over, I figured there was little chance I would ever see it again. I said I was sorry, but I just couldn't lend it. I had already packed my gear, so I swung my pack to my shoulders and headed home. After five minutes on the trail, God stopped me in my tracks.

In His gentle way, He smacked me on the head with Matthew 5:42, "Give to the one who asks you, and do not turn away from the one who wants to borrow from you." *Oh great,* I thought, *when He puts it that way, how can I argue? Sorry, Nate, no room for justifying this one!* I returned to the shelter where the Colorado men were still preparing for that day's hike. Addresses were exchanged, and my pack was a little lighter for my trip back to the car. I expected to be buying a new purifier in a few weeks.

Two weeks later, a package arrived at my apartment. Inside the small box was my water purifier! The note inside stated that the trip had been a success, and they were very grateful for my help. As I sat there holding the equipment, I realized that we are all in need of the One who can purify us. We cannot pass through this world in purity of heart without Him. Taking it a step farther, we don't need pure hearts and minds just for the sake of being clean, but we need to have them for the sake of others. Those three hikers needed me to have a pure heart so their expression of need wouldn't fall on deaf ears. And I needed God's cleansing so I could walk in obedience! Make this your prayer!

Create in me a pure heart, O God. Take away all my impurities so that I can be clean before You and a refreshment to others. In Jesus' name, amen.

16

Slow but Sure

At once they left their nets and followed Him.

Matthew 4:20

Today we can cover 70 miles in one hour very easily in a car. Planes moving along at 600 miles per hour are no big deal. But on foot, to hike 15 miles in the mountains during one day is quite a feat. Is "faster" always better? Henry David Thoreau said:

> I have learned that the swiftest traveller is he that goes afoot. I say to my friend, Suppose we try who will get there first. The distance is thirty miles; the fare ninety cents. That is almost a day's wages....Well, I start now on foot, and get there before night....You will in the meanwhile have earned your fare, and arrive there some time tomorrow, or possibly this evening, if you...get a job in season....You will be working here the greater part of the day. And so, if the railroad reached round the world, I think that I should keep ahead of you.*

When we are hiking, "getting there" is not the exclusive reason for travel because there's too much to learn and appreciate along the way. The same can hold true for

---

* Henry David Thoreau, *Walden: Life in the Woods* (1854).

our Christian walks. Being with Jesus in heaven is the ultimate goal, but there is joy in the journey.

Today many of us are tempted to try faster and easier methods of following Jesus. Perhaps a new book comes out claiming that being close to Jesus doesn't have to involve sacrifice. Or a group promises instant relationship and fulfillment by following certain steps. Because our daily schedules are so hectic, we gladly hop on the fast train. Maybe without realizing it, we are saying to Jesus, "I know where You want me to be, but instead of walking with You, I'll meet up with You later." Tallying miles is not what Jesus wants. He wants us to take each step with Him, to talk to Him along the way, to discover the rich wisdom and deep love He offers. This takes time and effort. Following Jesus is the best part of the journey. Getting to where we need to be with God will happen much more quickly and more delightfully when we are walking with Him "on foot."

Lord Jesus, just like the disciples left their ships and walked with You, help me follow You each step of the way. Keep me close by Your side on the journey. In Your name I pray, amen.

17

The Challenge

Consider it pure joy, my brothers, whenever you face
trials of many kinds, because you know that
the testing of your faith develops perseverance.

James 1:2,3

Hikers thrive on hardship. Just think about the nature of backpacking—we intentionally take ourselves out of comfort and into a vagabond life. A very experienced hiker once told me that the only difference between a backpacker on the trail and a homeless person is the $2500 of fancy clothes and impressive gear.

Tough terrain also makes our trips exciting. As long as we can stay dry and warm, we don't mind an occasional thunderstorm or snowdrift. Actually, the trips I remember most include something that was radically difficult.

Why does hardship make hiking more enjoyable? It provides interesting stories to tell and great learning opportunities. When things go wrong we also gain confidence in our hiking abilities. Never facing a challenge means never being tested. Without tests, we can't know or develop our abilities. But what about the tests that arise in our daily lives? Why do we resist those challenges? Perhaps because of the risk level. Our reputations, financial futures, and happiness could be affected. But James tells us to face trials with joy so we can attain maturity in our faith. Like Paul the apostle, says, "We know that in all things God works for the good of those who love him, who have been called according to his purpose" (Romans 8:28).

"Consider it all joy" is much easier on a trail than in a trial, but the end results for both areas of struggle are strength, vivid memories, and the ability to cope better the next time.

Heavenly Father, give me the proper attitude toward hardship. Thank You for the challenges in this life. Help me realize the lessons and strength You want me to have. In Your Son's name I pray, amen.

18

Together in the Journey

But if you show favoritism, you sin and are convicted by the law as lawbreakers.
James 2:9

When you're on the trail, you look forward to spending the evening at a shelter resting and visiting with other folks. And like anywhere else, people are quick to judge others. In hiking circles, the guy with the most expensive and newest gear is usually thought of as the most inexperienced. Old, tattered gear is considered a sign of years of hiking and a wealth of knowledge and experience. It's also hard to *not* notice the "styles" of other hikers. Some bring all the amenities while others bring very little. But we really don't know the backgrounds of other hikers without interacting with them. There *is* a moment in the shelter when none of this matters—dinnertime.

When the time comes to break out that long-awaited meal, everybody belongs. Some of my favorite memories are times when a random crowd of trekkers and I prepare dinner together and exchange jokes and stories. The "just add water" meals become the feasts of kings when camaraderie exists. The faces that strained while bringing 60 pounds up switchbacks and around fallen trees beam with laughter and fellowship.

This sense of community is very important on the trail and in our Christian walks. Exchanges between sojourners—especially within the body of Christ—are not luxuries; they are necessities.

Around the glow of a campfire and in the practices of Christianity, everyone needs to belong. *Every Christian* has a place around God's campfire. Sometimes those of us who travel light become prideful and less compassionate to those who carry large burdens because of all the amenities. Treating hikers differently based on their gear is a ludicrous activity that would break down the "hiking community" that is so needed for the journey.

The words from James 2:9 encourage us to treat everyone equally. When we trek with Jesus, we all find a place at His table regardless of our social position, financial status, or physical abilities. As we pause during our shared mealtime, we glance at the smiling faces of others who have chosen this place of peace. We share stories and encourage each other as we rest in God's presence.

Are you walking the narrow way? Are you accepting of others who are also on the journey? The body of Christ is one—Christians together in all the struggles and all the victories.

Lord Jesus, help me offer acceptance to all who enter the shelter of Your grace. I pray for friends who will not judge me based on what my "gear" looks like. Help me see people through Your eyes. I ask this in Your name, amen.

19

Waiting for Dawn

When Jesus spoke again to the people, he said,
"I am the light of the world. Whoever follows me
will never walk in darkness, but will have the light of life."

John 8:12

Have you found nighttime on the trail to be considerably longer than when you are at home? I remember the first time I experienced this phenomena. After a long day of rigorous hiking, I could hardly stay awake. The day's journey had zapped me completely, and I longed to crawl into my sleeping bag even though it was only 4:30 in the afternoon. It felt great to close my eyes, and I was grateful the forest was quiet. There was just me, the cool mountain wind, and the warmth of my 20-degree bag.

At 4:30 in the morning, I woke up with a start and looked at my watch. I was totally confused until I realized I had slept for 12 wonderful hours. I was completely awake, but the sunrise was a lingering two-and-a-half hours away. My body was ready to get up and start hiking, but that seemed a sketchy thing to do under the cover of darkness. I tried to get back to sleep, but instead I stared out into the darkness. I began to hear every movement of the critters that were stirring in the night. The next few hours tested my patience and my nerves.

Through each of those early-morning minutes, I realized my need for the light of the sun. And when it finally arrived, my entire surroundings came to visible life. Squirrels started their daily gathering, the birds' morning music sounded like joy, and the dark wall of the unknown was transformed into intricately detailed patterns of evergreens, fallen trees, and yellow flowers. I was watching a painting emerge from a black canvas. This night was finally over.

Waiting for the morning light is universal because we need it for sustenance and energy. But the greater need is for the *eternal* dawn—Jesus Christ.

Unfortunately, too many people see Jesus as just a part of history or an aspect of a religion. But He is much, much more than a name that appears on a "great leaders of the world" list. He is the light of the world. For those who accept this truth, life begins in Christ each day. It is in Him that darkness is dispelled so we can rise and journey through this life. It is in the light of Christ that the full, detailed beauty of life can be seen in our relationships, charity, human longings, mercy, and more.

As you zip your tent door closed tonight and settle in for your needed rest, remember that darkness is an unavoidable aspect of living day to day. But, in time, the sun will come again. When it does, rejoice in the light of Jesus.

Thank You, Jesus, for being the light of my world. I'm glad Your light never dims. Help me stay close to You so that my heart will never travel in darkness alone. In Your name I pray, amen.

20

Clear Reception

My sheep listen to my voice;
and I know them, and they follow me.
John 10:27

For safety's sake, most hikers carry a small radio to listen to weather reports. Otherwise a deceivingly beautiful and clear morning can catch us off guard when a storm suddenly hits. Reception on the trail is usually pretty good. One time on a mountain in southern Virginia, my dad and sister listened to a Christian radio station from Chicago! Mt. Roger's summit had taken them to an altitude where radio signals flowed free and clear.

When I lived in a small town near the Appalachian Trail, I was a mere 20 minutes from some of the best hiking and kayaking in the world. And there were national forests nearby. It was the ultimate in outdoor convenience. The only problem was that the mountainous terrain interrupted radio waves.

I'm a big fan of talk radio, and the closest AM station that rushed all the big names to my area was in Chattanooga, about 45 minutes away. It was easy to get consumed with trying to tune in each day. I used to balance the radio on the back of the couch because it was often the only place in my apartment that offered sufficient reception. Even in that spot I could only faintly hear voices through the crackles, hums, and whistles that accompany a weak signal. Many times I'd get so frustrated that I had to shut the radio off.

Sometimes the voice of our Savior can be drowned out by the static of living in a fallen world. And when we get frustrated we are tempted to give up listening. When I'm hiking and backpacking there are fewer distractions on the mountaintops. Being "up there" helps my spirit reach above and beyond the things that separate me from God. But even there clear reception isn't guaranteed. Sometimes, high on a mountain and well above the chaos of the cities below, I still struggle to hear Him. It's hard to admit that communing with God outdoors is not always the cure-all for experiencing a weak spiritual signal. At those times I know I can't hear Him because I haven't taken the time to get my radio "heart" tuned to the right station.

There are other times when, like distorted radio waves, I'm afraid I won't hear God's voice correctly. But Jesus promises that we can recognize His voice!

Knowing and hearing the Lord's call are key elements for following in His path. Scripture encourages us to "tune Him in" and eagerly listen for Him. We need to make every effort to keep world distractions turned down in order to clearly hear His divine voice.

Being in the wilderness or on the trail is a great way to be in touch with God because phones, televisions, and the internet are usually not readily available. But even when we can't get to the mountains we can make sure our dial is tuned to Jesus.

Thank You, God, for constantly sending Your words to my heart. Help me to always be attentive to what You have to say. Keep my mind clear so that I can clearly hear Your voice. In Your name I pray, amen.

21

Our Fortress

As the mountains surround Jerusalem, so the LORD
surrounds his people both now and forevermore.
Psalm 125:2

Have you stood at a clearing on a high trail and gazed to the far horizon and there is nothing but mountains between? Rows of purple peaks easily rise above low clouds and the morning sun highlights golden ridgelines with jagged edges that exude intimidating beauty. While gazing at a view like this, a sense of isolation comes over me—not the kind that produces fear or apprehension, but the kind that makes me feel safe, in control, and free from the tethers of modern society. It's not so much that I can't reach a phone to call my work, but more that they can't use a phone to reach me.

When I can tuck myself away in the forest, the surrounding mountains offer serenity. I am hidden for a while from the onslaught of the cares of life. In Psalm 125, David expresses this same delight in God's sanctuary. A mountain range in those days was a natural fortress that provided protection from enemies. David did not have to toil to make his refuge, God created it. You and I can also find God's love and protection by living in the middle of His will and presence.

When we look out over a mountainscape, it's easy to understand the elation and security of being deep in the middle of nature. The surrounding towers seem strong and immovable—like the protection and love God offers His children. As often as possible enjoy the surrounding beauty of a deep hike into the mountains. Daily be comforted and encouraged knowing you are surrounded by the Lord. He will keep you safe.

Thank You, Lord, for Your protection, for surrounding me with Your love and mercy. Help me stay in a place where I can be encompassed by Your will. In Your name I pray, amen.

22

Broken Stick, Broken Temper

A patient man has great understanding,
but a quick-tempered man displays folly.
Proverbs 14:29

Hiking trips don't always go as planned. Maybe we forget an important article of clothing or pack way too much. Worse yet is when we make mistakes that affect our fellow hikers. Even small blunders on the trail can live a long time in our memories. There's one particular trip with my dad and sister that I seldom share because I can barely remember the beautiful overlooks and campsites. The three of us were on a major hiking loop we had planned that required pretty intense altitude changes and rough terrain. We were forced to rely on our hiking sticks for support during the steep climbs and descents. Needless to say, we were all very tired by the end of the trip.

For the last two miles of our trek, we hiked through a winding area of low forest, and the going was easy. Dad and I had traded hiking sticks because his consisted of a couple of broom sticks with padding and duct tape for handles and I wanted him to use my much more pricey pole so he could experience the benefits of "high-tech" gear. We were running late for lunch, and my hunger, fatigue, and impatience were rising to the surface. I had been dreaming about pancakes the night before, and I was getting very irritated with our tardiness and the seemingly never-ending trail. I trudged along with my hat pulled low to avoid any interaction. The only conversation I wanted to have was between me and a stack of flapjacks.

Deep in pouting mode, I wasn't paying attention so I missed the fact that a large vine hung across the path. Dad pushed the vine over his head and walked on, assuming that his experienced hiker son was paying attention. The large vine connected with my hat just above the brim. Needless to say, the hat didn't offer my head much protection. The next think I knew, my head was ringing and I was seeing stars. Angry, I turned and saw a small tree next to the path. I swung Dad's cheap hiking stick against it. The three of us watched as, in slow motion, the bottom half of the stick went spinning into the darkness of the forest. I could tell from their horrified looks that my dad and sister were appalled. The only thing Dad said was, "Nate, promise me you'll never do that again." His quiet rebuke went straight to my heart. While a simple hiking stick can be replaced, I realized my uncontrolled temper caused me to lose something that could not be replaced—some of Dad's respect.

When I read today's proverb, I can see that my father's response and my actions exhibited "part one" and "part two." This was really driven home when I later learned that Dad called his hiking sticks "memory sticks." He told me that for years he used those same sticks on every trip. He had planned on using them throughout his hiking career to keep his footing and his memories all at the same time.

Dad's old hiking sticks have a resting place on his study wall. He now uses high-tech poles that my sister and I bought for him. I know he forgave me on the spot when I broke his stick, but even so a haunting memory of hurting my father keeps my eyes forward, my anger in check, my dependence on my heavenly Father as I travel through life's twists and turns.

Dear Lord, forgive me when I fail to hold my temper in check. Keep me patient and aware of how I should react to the obstacles that arise on life's path. Thank You for Your mercy, which reminds me to extend grace to others. I give my heart to You today, Lord. Amen.

23

Why Am I Here?

*Surely goodness and love will follow me all the days of my
life, and I will dwell in the house of the LORD forever.*

Psalm 23:6

Whenever I'm mindlessly devouring a prepackaged camper's meal or trying to get warm and comfortable in my tent, I always hear the voices of my mother and my wife. When their words echo in my head, I long for home. I can hear my mom saying, "Nathan, my door is always open. I am always ready to make a hot meal for you and your wife. Just call me and I'll start a cookin'!" As I lick my lips in want, I stop and wonder what am I doing so far from her table. When I shiver in my cold sleeping bag, I replay an exchange I had with my wife before we were married. When she commented she was cold, I gave her a hiker's response: "You can't always be warm, Babe." She responded, "No, but I can try!" The echo of her unwillingness to intentionally live with chills haunts me as I long for the warmth of her arms.

These scenarios play in my mind when I am eating meals that seem less than real food and my bed is nothing more than a dirty sleeping bag on the hard, cold ground. At these times I miss my family...but I choose to be here. I could pack up and go home to my wife for a warm meal and cozy evening. Stephanie and I could have dinner at Mom's. I always try to remind myself that I don't *have* to be here, but there is a benefit to what I'm doing. I love to hike.

In our Christian walks, the scenarios can look much the same. God is waiting and willing to bless us with the good things of this world. He longs for us to dwell in His house. But sometimes we choose to live in the forest. We live without faith, we ignore the promises of God, and we disobey His Word.

On the trail, we deprive ourselves for the fun and challenge of being out there in the wild. When we choose to live away from God's open door, we've usually confused instant gratification with true joy. This is a grave risk. I can encourage you to take hiking trips throughout the year, but I would never recommend living one moment away from the blessings of God. Leaving His protection, covering, and provision invites eternal consequences.

If you are out in a cold, ominous forest of spiritual rebellion, return to Jesus!

Lord Jesus, thank You that I can always come home to You. Help me rest in the safety of Your arms and the nourishment You provide through Your Word. I love You and need Your comfort. In Your name I pray, amen.

24

Just Enough

I have learned the secret of being content in any
and every situation, whether well fed or hungry,
whether living in plenty or in want.

Philippians 4:12

I have a ritual I go through before each trip. I take all
my gear and lay it out on the floor so I can make sure I
have everything and check each piece. My core equipment includes:

Gear
- wool socks
- rain pants
- poncho
- synthetic underwear
- hat
- gloves
- jacket
- sleeping bag
- ground pad
- tent
- stove and fuel
- water purifier and
  bottles
- boots
- journal
- Bible
- headlamp
- food
- bathroom items

Food
- powdered Tang
- instant coffee
- granola bars
- energy bars
- oatmeal
- prepackaged dinners

Luxuries
- extra book
- extra underwear
  and socks
- camera

For a weeklong trip, my pack usually weighs around 45 pounds to start and as little as 38 pounds at the end. My load is light compared to what I've seen others pack—everything from bagels and cream cheese to canned spaghetti sauce. My basic policy is that a luxury equals a burden. However, there are times when I do add pounds to my pack in order to share with others. Although I delight in being able to log the miles by being light, I also like to see the smiles of folks when I share my excess. Either way, I can be content. At the end of the day, whichever way I packed, I've had a good workout. If the long miles don't drain me, the heavy load takes its toll.

Is this the secret to Paul's statement in today's verse? Both types of hiking have advantages. Neither is better than the other. I believe it's the same in life. People with luxury items may have more cars to maintain and a bigger yard to mow—but they also have more to share with others. And, just as admirable, those of us who have little may accomplish more for Christ because our energies are streamlined and we have fewer distractions.

How do you pack? Heavy or light? Are you content?

Thank You, God, for Your variety of travelers. Help me serve You and others to the best of my abilities. Tell me when You want me to "pack light" or "pack heavy." In Your name I ask this, amen.

25

The Miracle of Hiking

*Very early in the morning, while it was still dark,
Jesus got up, left the house, and went off
to a solitary place, where he prayed.*

Mark 1:35

When the news came, it struck me hard. It hit me in the chest and left me reeling. Amy had died. She was my cousin who was only 13 years old. Because my mom was staying with her while she passed, my grandmother was keeping Heidi and me. While Grandmother was speechless, standing there in the kitchen, I turned and walked out the door. I didn't stop for quite some time.

My ten-year-old legs pumped as tears and bewilderment swelled up from deep within. I knew Amy had suffered and was now in a better place. Still, I missed her.

Reflecting back on that journey, I realize my time spent wandering the neighborhood was something God gave to me. There was a divine purpose behind my seeking solitude. In those moments spent on a concrete trail, God eased the pain in my heart. When I returned to Heidi and Grandma, I'd reconciled the sorrow and joy in my ten-year-old fashion.

Have you noticed that Jesus also took time to get away from everyone? Usually He hiked in the mountains while He talked with His Father. Although we don't know the words of Jesus during His alone time, we do know His days were filled with the reality of His mission on Earth and the impending death He faced. Jesus took the issues of the sins of the world to a solitary place in the surrounding hills and mountains. He carried these extra-large burdens to places of prayer and peace.

If your next hiking trip follows a time of hurting or if the burdens of this life seem too much to bear, be assured that Jesus is with you. While your back may feel the physical weight that presses down on your shoulders of flesh, the burdens of your heart are lifted when you seek God in the mountains. God will use the time on the trail to strengthen and renew your heart.

Heavenly Father, You know the load I am carrying right now. You understand the weight of my pain. Please take away my burdens and give my heart rest in You. Thank You, Father. I ask this in Your Son's name, amen.

Rest Is Not an Option

Observe the Sabbath day by keeping it holy,
as the LORD your God has commanded you.
Deuteronomy 5:12

My friend Eric and I entered the forest with full knowledge of what lay before us. We knew there was a 3,000-foot climb in the first 3 miles of this 10-mile day with a total of 4,500 feet to ascend. Ouch! That fact was tough enough to deal with, but there was another bit of information that bothered me more: Eric was in much better shape than I was.

During the previous semester in college, I had logged 18 hours per week in class, 7 hours per week as an assistant teacher, 5 hours per week in guitar practice, and 20 hours per week in my studies. Every one of those 50 hours were sedentary. Eric, however, had maintained a rigorous training schedule on his mountain bike. While he was looking forward to the exhilaration of the climb, I was dreading the pain.

We started off at a fast pace, and I followed his lead. I was surprised, but I felt great—even after the first 3 miles! I maintained a strenuous clip for quite some time; however, I was soon asking God to give me strength so that I could keep up. I desperately wanted to have some dignity left at the end of the day…but then mile 9 came.

Although it was a much easier grade, I was without a thread of energy. At this point, I had no pride left either. I had to stop over and over again. My thigh muscles were twitching and cramping. I could walk only a few steps before my legs would stop moving. I apologized each time. I began to think that Eric was really a robot—no human could be so fit. It was very humbling.

During those moments of feeling so low while high on a mountain, I had a revelation. If I had been willing to stop and rest for a few minutes early on, then my body wouldn't have shut down the way it did. I was forced to stop and rest because of self-inflicted pain and pride.

After that experience, the concept of Sabbath took on new meaning. God has not designed us to always be on the go. He included in our humanity the need to rest. For the Israelites, resting one day a week was a reminder that they were no longer slaves and who had delivered them. Resting each week helped them keep in mind their own humanity and their covenant with God.

As I discovered, being obedient to God in the area of rest requires humility and obedience. I was too full of pride to ask Eric for a few moments of rest earlier in that fateful day and I paid the price. We need to lay down our pride in our daily lives to remain faithful to God's command so we can accomplish all God has planned for us. For some of us, the difference between resting and not resting may determine whether we drive a Taurus or a Mercedes or whether we live in a mansion or a two-bedroom apartment. If we work so hard that we miss special times with friends, family, and the Lord, these relationships won't be as strong as they could be.

On the hike my penalty for being too prideful to rest was merely aching legs. For life as a whole, the cost can be far more serious. Shallow relations with God and others, fatigue that breaks down the immune system, and an early trip to the grave are a few consequences we could encounter.

If you're hiking today or racing through life, don't forget the benefits of taking time to rest. One day each week was all God required of the Israelites. Surely we can handle that!

Lord Jesus, it's so hard to really rest. Please ease the anxiety in my heart that sends me to work when I shouldn't be there. Remind me that Your plan includes rest. Help me never forget that You did a work here on Earth that provides real rest— physically and spiritually. Thank You. In Your name, amen.

27

Whose Glory Is It?

*For the LORD your God is bringing you into
a good land—a land with streams and pools of water,
with springs flowing in the valleys and hills.*

Deuteronomy 8:7

There is a moment in hiking that is especially pleasurable—boot removal. At the end of a long, hard hike, my dogs are whimpering and aching, and there is nothing else in this world like loosening the laces, letting the boots plop down on the forest floor, and peeling off the stinky, steamy socks that have the displeasure of hugging my feet all day. My body aches with the physical pain of the day, but when my fine leather investments finally retreat, a wave of accomplishment sweeps over my soul.

We experience this in daily life, too. At the end of a long day at work—tie and dress shoe removal, and for the ladies—high heel removal. At the end of a hard day at school—backpack removal. At the end of a day full of appointments and worry—watch removal.

For a long time I thought I deserved the feelings of accomplishment that came with "removals." I thought the thousands of little activities that day were mine so I was the person who should be congratulated for what I had accomplished that day. Now I see things differently.

First, I am a created being. The fact that I exist is not to my credit. Second, God has given me every ounce of strength for all I've ever finished in this life. Finally, without God I would be so miserable I could not even begin to enjoy finishing a task—at home, at work, or on the trail. God certainly took the children of Israel to their land of peace and prosperity. This miracle was visible— their food and water were provided while they were in the desert. For us, it can be harder to notice that God is behind any accomplishment or credit we call our own.

On the trail, we struggle to traverse mountains, but we are using legs created by Him. Those mountains we climb were created by Him, and they tremble in His presence. As we walk through life, we might wear the boots but *He* wears the crown.

God, I give my accomplishments to You. You are the beginning and end of my existence on this earth. I acknowledge that right now. In Jesus' name I pray, amen.

28

The Secret Room

When he thunders, the waters in the heavens roar;
he makes clouds rise from the ends of the earth.
He sends lightning with the rain and brings
the wind from his storehouses.
Jeremiah 10:13

At high altitudes, the sky seems like a low ceiling you could touch with an outstretched hand. After a long hike, part of the pain in returning to civilization is that the blue of the sky loses its intensity and the intimate clouds become estranged and far away. But beautiful days near the top of a mountain are not the only times of high wilderness wonder. Perhaps the most amazing times to be atop a far-reaching peak are the minutes just before a storm hits.

Such was the case for my friend and me on top of a mountain, around 5,800 feet. A storm started to blow in. The wind became cold and unfriendly. The trees swayed back and forth doing side-bends, desperately reaching for the forest floor. The sky the day before had been beautiful but ordinary. Today, the contrast between ominous dark clouds and brilliant streaks of sunlight made the sky like a scene from an Edgar Allen Poe story. We were not filled with fear; instead a deep respect swept through our beings.

Eric was the first to speak. "I feel like we have stumbled into the secret room where the weather is made. Like we are watching the storm clouds being formed. Maybe we shouldn't be here."

As we continued walking, we marveled at God's power and His creation. And that's what hiking is all about. Far below the ridgeline where Eric and I trekked, the impending bad weather was a nuisance or a report between commercials on a car radio. But here it was real, mysterious, and awe-inspiring. We walked where the action was. We hugged the side of the mountain with our ponchos flapping around our legs as the rain made our hands and faces cold. God was actively making an impressive display out of weather. And we were right there!

A few weeks later, I came across Jeremiah's description of a storm. It seemed so similar to what I had experienced that I was struck by a freshness and understanding I hadn't known before. Eric and I had felt the foreboding power of the brewing squall. But what amazed me in today's verse was the reminder that God was the source behind the tempest.

When we walk through life we often sense the approach of trials. But whatever appears on the horizon, as long as we stay close to God our lives will include a beauty and wonder that can't be seen or felt by those who are far away from Him. The apostle Paul sang in prison, Joseph dreamed dreams in captivity, and Samson grew strong in blindness. Why? Because these guys were right where the action was. They didn't have it easy; they didn't avoid storms. They experienced the secret room where God starts things and followed God's paths which led where His will is implemented. They followed God. That's what I want to do.

On that stormy day on the mountain, I looked down and realized that both the righteous and unrighteous get rained on. But Eric and I had front-row seats to witness and acknowledge God's awesome power.

Lord Jesus, help me stay close by Your side today. I want to be where the action is. I want to stay in Your will—it is the only safe place I know. Thank You for walking with me through the storms of life. In Your name I pray, amen.

29

The Compass

They refused correction. They made their faces
harder than stone and have refused to repent.
Jeremiah 5:3

Deep in a thickly wooded forest, it is easy to get
turned around. The trees and tall shrubs form high,
impenetrable walls that don't let even a thin shaft of light
shine through. In these conditions, a map and compass
are as valuable as a diamond during a marriage proposal.

All hikers have "when I got lost" stories. Mine is
rather embarassing. I was on my way back to my truck
when I realized I didn't know if the red side or white side
of the compass was north! I finally found my way out of
the woods, but I had to walk down a few trails to get
there. The whole time I had my compass, so I would at
least look like I knew what I was doing. Ever heard squirrels laughing? I have.

All of us who have gotten lost can relate to the desperate yearning to turn and know we're starting in the
right direction. There is no loss of pride, no shame,
merely a deep jubilation knowing our steps are taking us
closer to our destination.

In the book of Jeremiah, God offered Israel the
opportunity to repent or, if they didn't, face much suffering. The choice between God's grace and His judgment was before them. However, God's children were not

willing to turn around. They were rebelling against repentance. What is incredibly interesting is that the word "repent" is based on the Hebrew word *shuwb*, which means "to turn." For the Israelites, it was that simple— turn. But with their faces set like stone, they stubbornly said no to God's correction, ensuring that the judgment that was promised would surely come.

The Israelites' rock-hard refusal to yield in repentance causes me to examine my own heart and ask a hard question: Am I willing to endure the judgment that would come upon me if I set my face against God? No! Heaven is my ultimate hiking destination. I may get disoriented from time to time, but in no way do I want to get forever lost. Repentance is my compass.

Thank You, Lord, for loving me even though You know I sometimes refuse to heed Your call. Help me, right now, to make "the turn." In Your name I pray, amen.

30
Don't Look Down

Direct my footsteps according to your word;
let no sin rule over me.
Psalm 119:133

The night before our longest day during a through-hike in the Smoky Mountains, Eric and I eagerly listened to the weather report on my small radio. Over a serving of freeze-dried spaghetti, we heard that rain was coming. This was an especially bad report because the ice and snow covering the trail were already making it difficult to continue.

The next day a midmorning storm blew in, and the trail reacted. It got really nasty, and the ice turned to an ugly slush. But just before it did that we experienced the most treacherous part of our excursion.

At around 5,500 feet, we were hiking ridgelines with dropoffs that descended for hundreds of feet on either side of the trail. The terrain was taking us higher and higher, and many times we were climbing stair-stepped miniature switch-backs that were covered with ice. Once, and only once, I turned around to catch a view. It was then that I fully realized I was one unsure step away from following my pack in a backward dive toward the treetops far below. In that moment of instant terror, my footing became my chief concern. Nothing else was on my mind.

Finishing a successful hike, seeing my family again, and avoiding permanent injury depended on how carefully I chose my path. Even with crampons, the going would have been treacherous. As Eric and I ice skated over the Smoky Mountain ridges, we had to concentrate so the peaks wouldn't "have dominion" over us. One moment of taking our eyes off the trail or a lapse in concentration would have created a headline neither of us wanted to read.

Dealing with this kind of danger was something King David undoubtedly understood. From his days of running from King Saul, hiding out in caves, and waging war in lands beyond the hills of Jerusalem, we can be sure David knew a thing or two about hiking in the mountains. He reveals that he was aware of the beauty of the peaks—and the danger that lurked in them. He knew a foolish slip in his daily existence would cost him much more than he wanted to pay. Drawing on his climbing experience, the psalmist was well aware of the importance of taking every step carefully.

Today we hear stories with dismal endings often—a pastor confesses to an affair, a Christian is caught embezzling funds. We are hardly shocked anymore, but we should be. God *wants* to direct us. He *wants* us to walk with Him and lead others to Jesus.

It takes only one side-glance or one wayward thought, and the ice of sin is the winner.

Dear Lord, establish my footsteps in Your Word. Keep me safe and help me stay in Your will, amen.

31
The Divine Loop

*So in everything, do to others
what you would have them do to you.*
Matthew 7:12

My father refuses to place much trust in gas gauges. He believes the orange light on the dash shaped like a gas pump is merely a suggestion, not a warning. It's as though the red-lined fuel needle is saying that if you feel like it and all the conditions are favorable, then getting gas might be a good idea—if not, then that's cool, too! Needless to say, he has lost a few times. Several times I watched my dad's silhouetted form as he trucked off into the distance looking for a nearby exit...and a friendly face and a service station. A little while later, he would return with a can of gas and a smiling Samaritan behind the wheel of an old, bumper-lacking truck.

When I go hiking, the foot trip I take bears a close resemblance to Dad's fuel hunts...minus the out-of-gas part. When I head off into the forest, I usually make a huge circle through the hills and return to my truck, or I go in one direction and then take a vehicle back to my own. An aerial view of my dad's hikes and mine would not look much different: Two men get out of their cars, walk somewhere carrying a load, walk back, get in their cars, and drive off. Hmmm.

So what *is* the difference? Attitude. Most unexpected day hikes are unwelcome. They yank us out of our routine and force us to put our lives on hold until a problem is solved.

But that's what so great about hiking—it takes us away from the daily grind. We appreciate planned diversions through the forest; the unplanned ones can make us extremely stressed.

When life takes us off the beaten path, sometimes we also panic and dig in our heels. Maybe God puts a burden on our hearts to give someone a ride. God asks us to go out of our way to help someone. It is a sad fact that even Christians can justify taking a week-long cruise before taking an extra fifteen minutes on our way home from church to serve God. But the unplanned loop may be from God!

From walking on a stormy sea to get to His scared disciples to stopping along the road as He entered a city to raise a widow's only dead son, Jesus knew about unexpected "day trips." He endured them because He cared about the people. I want to be like that, too. I want to be willing to take unplanned trips to help others. If God provides the map, the road will always lead back to Him. It's the divine loop.

Jesus, help me imitate Your willingness to change plans for the needs of others. Help my attitude concerning the unexpected day hikes that are part of daily living. Thank You for the chance to walk with You—whatever the path, wherever it leads. In Your name I pray, amen.

32

Stephanie's Charge

But our citizenship is in heaven. And we eagerly await a Savior from there, the Lord Jesus Christ.
Philippians 3:20

Twenty-five miles left. When Eric and I started our trip, we had 70 miles to go. We covered 45 miles in five days. It had been that many days since I had talked to Stephanie. I ached to see my fiancée and hoped she had a serious longing to see me. With that in mind I began to coerce Eric into a crazy idea. "Maybe we'll push ourselves and get out of the mountains by tomorrow," I enthused Then I used food as the motivator.

"We'll call it 'Ryan's Charge,'" I suggested. "Don't you want Ryan's? Mmmmm!" (For those of you who don't know, Ryan's is a restaurant chain that features a smorgasbord of hot, colorful, fresh food...steak...prepared by someone else.) "Aren't you hungry, Eric?" I went on. "Wouldn't you love to feel full again? I haven't felt satisfied since leaving the truck. How about you, ol' buddy?"

Finally my coaxing got to him. He started repeating the words "Ryan's Charge." He didn't know I was secretly calling it "Stephanie's Charge." I missed her so badly and realized again how much my long-distance significant other sustained me. I felt my hunger-ridden heart starting to weep. I love the forest, but it doesn't love me back the way Stephanie does. I was ready to go. As we hiked I whispered silently, "I'm on my way, Steph!"

The next morning at 6:00, I was out of my bag waking Eric. Within minutes, we were ready to hit the trail. We hiked and hiked…and hiked…and hiked until I actually thought I had broken one of my legs because the pain was so awful. The last four miles of our longest day was an elevation drop of 3,000 feet. Yeow! The only comfort I could find was in repeating, "I'm on my way, Babe!"

Maybe it was because I accidentally thought those words out loud. I'm not sure how, but somewhere along the way Eric figured out why I was so driven. Why I was so eager to burn all the calories to ensure the promise of finding a phone that evening. Why I was giving away things such as stove fuel to other hikers and dumping Tang on the ground to lighten my load for the sake of swiftness. But the pain…it was excruciating. Perhaps the worst I've experienced with a pack on. We could barely walk when we got back to his truck.

When I realized he had put it all together, I knew I had to make amends for being so manipulative. I tried to appease him by promising to buy his dinner. I told him I was willing to do anything to get back to Stephanie. So I paid for a hotel room where we could shower and get a good night's sleep. The next morning I bought him breakfast. As we drove home he sat in the truck and moaned in pain…and mumbled something to the effect, "That's what I get for hiking with an engaged guy!"

Today's Scripture shines for me because of that hike. If Stephanie is a picture of the church that looks eagerly for Christ's coming (and she was indeed anxious to see me!), then I was the snapshot of the coming groom. I sacrificed so much that it hurt to make the journey to my sweetheart's side. But Jesus sacrificed far more to reach us! Then it dawned on me. *He must look forward to seeing us as much as we want to see Him!* That thought can make any sore muscle feel better—don't you agree?

Thank You, Lord Jesus, for the sacrifice You made on the cross. It surpasses any sacrifice I can ever make. I am eager to see You face to face. Please come soon. In Your name I pray, amen.

33

Looking Up?

And all our righteous acts are like filthy rags.

Isaiah 64:6

On a cool, March evening, I stepped outside my tent to brush my teeth before bed. I was camped at 5,000 feet, and the sky was clear and glittered like a country music sportscoat on the stage of the Grand Ole Opry. Even Porter Wagoner would have been jealous of the stars twinkling and dancing in the sky. The treetops seemed to scrape the edges of the brilliant nighttime light show. Never in the city do I see skies that even come close to this brilliance.

As I poured a little water onto my toothbrush before brushing, I was also enamored with my headlamp I had purchased just before leaving town. Powered by only two AAA batteries, its halogen design was amazing, and it flooded the area around my feet with an incredibly strong wash of white light. The novelty of this new gadget distracted me from my late-night enjoyment of the stars above. I started moving my head around to see how far the beam would go. Anything close got a good painting of its illumination. The tree trunks and wooden outhouse nearby stood out like it was daytime.

I decided to look up one more time before returning to the shelter. However, this time, having a new awareness of my headlamp, I actually thought, *Oh, I wonder if I'll still be able to see the stars with my headlamp on.* What was I thinking? How could a manmade object outshine God's incredible creation. As I focused on God's awesome power, I realized that when we do good deeds and try to be righteous before God, it is the same as thinking we can drown out the brilliant lights of heaven with a little headlamp. As today's Scripture reveals, even our best efforts fail. Our little headlamps of attempted righteousness can't compete with the glory of heaven.

The next time you're standing in the darkness of this world, look to the heavens and see the sparkling, distant beauty of God's righteousness. Remember that even the best headlamps can't outdo the stars. We need the light of Jesus to shine.

Lord, the righteousness You expect is impossible to obtain on my own. I ask that You see me through what Jesus did on the cross. Please forgive me for thinking I could possibly do anything good that would shine like Your light from heaven. I give You my weaknesses and faults right now, and praise Your name. In Your name I pray, amen.

34

The Path of Peace

He guides me in paths of righteousness for his name's sake. Even though I walk through the valley of the shadow of death, I will fear no evil, for you are with me.

Psalm 23:3,4

When the hiking trail takes a turn and leads to a quiet overlook, nothing in the world can disturb the peaceful pause that comes like a cool breeze in a warm sun. This moment is unique to the trail. For ages, writers have documented moments of peace in nature, but few have followed the path of serenity into dark valleys like the poet David did.

Why did he trace the path of righteousness into the valley of death? The psalmist knew that even when we follow closely behind God, sometimes the trails of this life lead into places filled with despair. But even in those situations David responded with a declaration of confident peace: "I will fear no evil."

When I walk through the high-ridge woods and river-bottom fields of North America, times of peace and renewal come often. However, along with those times are also moments of fear due to thunderstorms, lightning, intense cold, getting lost, extreme fatigue, and so on. But even with that, hikers walk on.

Sometimes following the path of righteousness leads us to where we don't want to go. Our ultimate goal is not to find "the path of least resistance," but to follow the path of God. On those same trails that lead us up and down steep mountains, through storms and hunger and cold, are also the beautiful afternoons spent with pen and journal, cool water, and delicious gorp. Good times and hard times on the trail are inseparable.

And in the same way, both the bitter and sweet times in life are on the same path. Thankfully, we know where this trail ends: "And I will dwell in the house of the LORD forever" (Psalm 23:6).

Lord Jesus, I will walk with You, even when I am led into times of hardship. Thank You for never leading me anywhere You haven't already been. I hike with You because You walked this earth and died here for me. I praise Your blessed name, amen.

35

The Never-Ending Peak

Blessed is the man who perseveres under trial, because when he has stood the test, he will receive the crown of life that God has promised to those who love him.

James 1:12

There is a particular north-to-south hike in the Smoky Mountains section of the Appalachian Trail that leads up to Mollies Ridge Shelter. The trail is steep and unforgiving. The ascent leads relentlessly higher and higher…almost to the clouds. At every turn, there is a new section to climb that was not visible before. I call this the "Mountain with the Never-Ending Peak."

Because the mountain does not follow a smooth grade all the way up, hiking it makes you feel like an ant climbing a giant staircase. Trekkers can see the peak just ahead, but behind the trees at every stage there is blue sky…and more mountain.

I found this succession of peaks to conquer quite frustrating and almost demoralizing. My emotions were creating a complex ridgeline system of their own. *I did it!* I'd think. Then came, *What? There's more?*

Every time I rounded a corner, I breathed a sigh of relief and expected to be at the peak. But on and on the climbing went. My brief climb extended to an hour. By the time I finally reached Mollies Ridge, my joy of finishing the climb was tainted by deep anger founded on all the disappointments of the many celebrations I had prematurely allowed.

In this one hour, I gained another snippet of wisdom that will help sustain me for the remainder of my days: The ascent to holiness is like that trail. One peak after another appears as God fine-tunes our faith.

In today's verse, James is writing about a consistent kind of perseverance, the type that drives us up the path of improvement. "Persevering" is by definition an ongoing pursuit, but receiving the crown of life is a one-time event. We strive to be holy for that moment when God will say, "Well done, good and faithful servant!" (Matthew 25:23).

If your pursuit of righteousness seems to be nothing but an uphill climb, be encouraged. This is the path God wants you on. He longs for Christians who are not afraid to take the trail all the way to the top. He'll hike alongside you and give you rest when you're weary. And the final reward is being with Him forever!

Jesus, thank You for going all the way to the top of the hill where You were lifted up on a cross. Thank You for persevering. Help me climb the mountains of righteous living and not turn back. In Your name I pray, amen.

36

Blisters at the Trailhead

My grace is sufficient for you.
2 Corinthians 12:9

Eric and I had our gear spread out on the tailgate of my truck. We were parked at a ranger station, about 20 minutes from starting a long springtime hike. However, there was one item Eric was taking that he desperately wanted to leave behind—a juicy, nickel-sized blister on his foot.

Eric had gone on a "preparation hike" the week before to help his body prepare for the tough hike ahead of us (we were planning an average of 15 miles a day). However, the consequence of his prehike was going to make things harder for him. He kept a log of our hike that week. For the first night's entry he wrote:

> I'm going to tape up my blister before I hike tomorrow. I can live with the pain, but I would rather not be distracted from all of the beauty. Enough medicine and mole-skin should do the trick.

Eric started his journey at a disadvantage because he was paying for his decision to wear textured cotton socks for his prehike jaunt. Now, facing days of rough terrain, he was expecting major foot discomfort. He was determined, in spite of the pain, to complete the journey.

I admired Eric's tenacity for not letting his blunder keep him from the trail, and it made me think of how many of us start our Christian journey with the blisters of poor decisions made before we met Christ. As Romans 3:23 tells us, "For all have sinned and fall short of the glory of God." Our presalvation transgressions leave welts and scars that cannot be ignored. We bring them to the trailhead of our Christian walk. Thankfully, Christ has the medical supplies for binding up our wounds.

What is in His divine first-aid kit? He doctors the blistered areas of our hearts with the salve of His forgiveness. He has plenty, and it never runs out. Then He covers our wounded hearts with His grace. To help us in future journeys, He teaches us what causes blisters. This information is vital so we can avoid their annoying return.

Because blisters and many other problems are a product of heat and friction. Jesus asks us to take care of our relationships. If there's stress between us and others, we are to extend kindness toward them. If they have offended us, we are told to forgive them like Jesus forgives us. Next, God's Word directs us to take off the smelly, rough garments of habits, greed, gossip, lust, and other blister-producing material. Once removed, He places the soft, smooth robe of His righteousness around us.

With God's remedies in place, and our new knowledge of how to keep the blisters away (or at least to a minimum), Jesus says, "Walk!" Whatever ails us when we come to the trailhead, God is there to heal our wounds—

even if they are self-inflicted. Don't let blisters keep you from starting your journey!

Thank You, Lord Jesus, for healing my wounded heart. I want to walk with You always. Thank You for letting me be part of Your journey. I love You and praise You. Amen.

37

A Sweet Diversion

The Lord is my shepherd…He restores my soul.
He guides me in paths of righteousness for his name's sake.
Psalm 23:1,3

While hiking under a canopy of clear blue skies and deep green treetops, I often look from right to left, constantly searching for one of those glorious scenes that can be found only thousands of feet above sea level. However, many times the ridgeline doesn't allow for side views. The trees and brush shield the spectacular view just beyond the wall of vegetation. Thus, sometimes a side trail is a very welcome diversion.

There is one such place on Mt. Camerer in the Great Smokies. The climb to the peak takes about four hours, but all that hard work is wasted if I don't take the side trail to the fire lookout. The side trail is .6 miles long, 1.2 miles roundtrip. But the view is awe inspiring.

There's something about side trails like this one that reminds me of what happens when I'm taking a daily walk through the Scriptures. I might be reading a familiar passage when suddenly a thought pulls me off the trail and leads me to a new revelation. One day I was passing through the glorious view of Psalm 23, a well-known trail for many souls. Suddenly, in verse three, I found myself side-trailed by the thought, *It is for His name's sake, not mine, that the Lord leads me in the paths of righteousness.* As I pondered the implications, I realized once again that the whole purpose for my journey to heaven is that God's name will be glorified. The trip is about Him, not me. All I do must be carefully considered so that Jesus' good name is protected. The farther I went down that side trail, the sweeter the realization became that I, a mere human, was entrusted with the opportunity to represent someone so eternally distinguished. I felt recharged in my soul to be His worthy ambassador.

Open God's Word and experience the incredible panorama of His truth. I guarantee you'll find some incredible views.

Lord God, as You lead me through Your Word today, please keep my heart soft and pliable so that I can see the glorious view You have for my heart right now. I will listen for what You have to say, even if it takes me off the main path. Thank You for leading me. In Your Son's name I pray, amen.

38

Act!

On the shaded side of the mountain stood a small log shelter. The darting beams of battery-powered lights created a miniature rock-n-roll light show while hungry guys and gals made after-sunset dinners. On this particular night, some of the hikers were not simply having a meal—these weekend warriors were having a party.

Eric and I lay in our sleeping bags trying to have a civil conversation amid the coarse jokes and foul language being bandied about. Some of the guys were passing a bottle back and forth, too. I knew how to deal with foxes and bears, but I had never encountered a "party" animal in the wild.

Alcohol consumption in backcountry is extremely dangerous. When someone is inebriated, he or she doesn't register true body temperature. A deceiving warmth is felt that often keeps the person from taking necessary precautions. Further, one of the most needed faculties in the mountains is an accurate sense of direction. Without these two major skills, a hiker is extremely vulnerable. That night a terrible tragedy was narrowly averted.

Around 1:30 in the morning, a disturbance in the shelter woke Eric and me up. One of the guys on the top level had decided to go outside to check on his buddy, who had foolishly decided to sleep outside the shelter in a camping hammock in 40-degree weather. When his friend found him, it was almost too late. The drunken hiker had gotten up and staggered off into the night. When his buddy found him, he was lying facedown in a stream. He had vomited and passed out. Hypothermia had set in and he was in danger of drowning.

When other campers got up to help, I stayed put, feeling very little compassion for the fellow who had given in to such irresponsible behavior. In fact, I didn't even unzip my sleeping bag. After everything settled back down and was quiet again, I thought of how I hadn't moved a muscle to help. I began to feel guilty and defeated. I had come up short in my Christian walk.

Although I had wisely turned down offers to drink and was cordial to the hikers who were keeping everyone awake, I failed to show the least bit of compassion to the one who had chosen the hammock hotel. Even though he nearly killed himself, my heart was hard. The sad truth hit home. I was no better than the party people because I was guilty of being inebriated by self-righteousness. Of all the people who should have been willing to lift another fallen soul, I should have been the first. Not because I was better, but because Jesus tells His followers to reach out to others.

Many months later, while listening to a sermon at church, I realized even more clearly how I had missed the mark that night in the woods. At that time I was thinking, *Mountain men have to survive; there's no mercy in the mountains.* However, James 2:17 doesn't specify criteria for helping others. The Scripture just says that if we have faith we will act. It's easy to give assistance to those who need help because of a natural disaster or a situation they had no control over. Helping those who find themselves in need because of poor judgment or different priorities challenges our compassion. But where would we be if others had that attitude when we needed mercy?

Since that night on the trail, I no longer sit back when others truly need help because it is an extension of my faith in Christ. How do you respond?

Thank You, Jesus, that someone had compassion on me during times of foolish choices. Please help me to be sensitive to others who need help along the way—even when they get themselves into trouble. In Your name I pray, amen.

39

The Chattanooga Boys

*Lot looked up and saw that the whole
plain of Jordan was well watered,
like the garden of the LORD, like the land of Egypt.*

Genesis 13:10

The morning sun triumphed. The night before had been my coldest night ever on the trail: 5 degrees Fahrenheit. Eric and I had decided that the weather was too bad for us to finish our 70-mile trip. More snow was supposed to be coming, which would add to the waist-deep drifts that were lounging on the ridgeline.

But the morning sun...it was beautiful. It looked like spring had sprung. Though we desperately wanted to press on, those dreaded words of wisdom whispered in our ears: *Turn back?* We made the tough decision. The radio was promising harder weather than we had already endured. We were five hours of hiking from the truck. Going back now meant safety and the assurance of spending Christmas with our families instead of being stranded in the wild. So we made the emotionally difficult way back.

About 11:30, at the height of the day's glorious beauty, Eric and I came upon three guys who were headed up the mountain and into the depths of the forest. We spotted a Rock Creek Outfitter's cap and knew they were from our area. When the "Chattanooga Boys" (as we later referred to them), met us, instead of meeting two cordial hikers from their hometown, they encountered two guys who were adamant about why they should do as we had done and turn back.

"It's gonna get bad," I said.

"You guys really ought to consider turning back. The weather is going to be terrible," said Eric.

"The weather's really supposed to turn," I added.

The other hikers looked at us as though we were mad. There we were, in 45 degrees of sunny springtime. They thought we were speaking nonsense; but we knew that the weather forecasters had predicted storms. Also, we had experienced the frightening cold the night before.

That evening, as Eric and I were trying to console ourselves that we were not wimps, we watched snowflakes the size of quarters fall with intense purpose. The temperature dropped to around 15 degrees. That meant that the mountaintops were going to have minus degree temperatures. We prayed for the Chattanooga boys and hoped they would turn back the next morning.

Even though Eric and I hiked back in beautiful weather, we knew the pleasant breeze and melting snow reflected the calm before the storm. The Chattanooga Boys were deceived by what seemed like a positive turn in the weather. The best decision had been to leave the forest. We set a parameter for making decisions and followed it. The appearance of the day mattered little based on the facts we knew.

In Old Testament days, Lot had a similar choice to make. He looked over the land and saw a beautiful countryside with financial promise. But looks were deceiving. He ended up in a violent land and had to flee from the city he lived in because it was destroyed by God.

If we aren't trusting God, sometimes the most beautiful paths lead us to places that turn bitterly cold. We need to be on guard and in constant communication with Jesus.

Lord, help me to make wise decisions. I'm seeking Your wisdom and Your will right now. In Your name I pray, amen.

40

Advanced Hiking

Then Peter got down out of the boat,
walked on the water and came toward Jesus.
Matthew 14:29

Being around other adventurers, I've heard of some amazing hikes. Campfire stories have included hikers covering incredible distances in short periods of time. For example, a few men have finished the 2,500-mile Appalachian Trail in only 6 weeks. (The average time is 5 to 7 months.) Other stories include surviving intense storms and encountering ferocious wildlife. And in books on mountaineering, I've read adventurous accounts of people climbing to the ceiling of the world on Mount Everest and K6. And, beyond the surface of the Earth, some men have hiked on the moon!

Sometimes, while hiking at a mere 5,000 feet, I imagine myself trudging through a Nepalese blizzard. On either side, the drop is one mile before jagged-edged rocks would stop my fall and I would suddenly feel no more. Or maybe the footsteps I'm taking are the ones in photographs just before the peak at 30,000 feet. A feeling of triumph would melt away the cold.

The feet of humans have touched some amazing places. Footprints remain where the world doubted that people could go. But nothing compares to the amazing hike the apostle Peter took one night on a lake. He was not at a high altitude. He was not moving quickly. He was not on a distant moon. There was a small storm, but the Bible depicts it as little more than high winds. So what was so special? He was hiking on top of deep water!

Now isn't that mind-boggling? I'm awestruck at the thought of it. Of all the hiking stories I've ever heard, it's hard to top that one. Peter did something more astounding than any other hiker could ever dream of. Even the guys on the moon can't top it. To walk on water defies every basic law of physics.

Sir Edmund Hillary. Neil A. Armstrong. Saint Peter. How did the simple fisherman from 2,000 years ago find himself in the same category with these great explorers? Simple—he was walking with Jesus.

Have you thought of any amazing expeditions you'd like to embark upon in the near future? You could make your mama sad by climbing Everest. You could spend a gazillion dollars going to the moon. But why not tackle the ultimate challenge—walk with Jesus.

Lord Jesus, help me to not pursue making a mark in this physical world. I want to walk with You. Thank You for a truly exciting and amazing journey. In Your name, I pray, amen.

41

Going in Circles

*A man can do nothing better than to eat
and drink and find satisfaction in his work.*
Ecclesiastes 2:24

Most great hikes of history follow the same route: a big circle. When people travel to Nepal to climb Everest, they leave from the same airport at which they arrived three months earlier. So why go to all the trouble? Remember how good a handful of peanuts served with cold water tastes on the trail? How about cold hands and a warm fire on a winter hike. How about a sunset glow at 6,000 feet. The beauty of the glow of the horizon is doubled as you remember each step taken to reach the scene. Your eyes are the lenses for what is usually seen only in magazines and photography books.

Hiking involves circles, and so does life. Our first few moments and our last few moments are more similar than we might think. We go from vulnerable to vulnerable. From helpless and unable to speak to helpless and unable to speak. From without possessions to without possessions. Solomon commented on this when he wrote, "All of it is meaningless" (Ecclesiastes 2:17). The circle itself is meaningless, but what is not is the effect the journey has on us.

When we hike, we encounter the limitations of this physical world. We don't *really* get anywhere because we move in circles. But what about our spiritual journey?

As we press forward in our spiritual walk, we have a destination. Heaven is our home. The path there is "straight and narrow" (see Proverbs 3:67; Matthew 7:13). We have a direct path to eternity.

Ecclesiastes 2:24 illustrates just how life moves forward and yet never takes us anywhere. All we can do is "eat and drink," then repeat it the next day. The sport of hiking is an excellent illustration of this. We certainly eat, and we most definitely drink (a creek's worth of water, for me), and we find great satisfaction in strapping on our packs and hitting the trail every day. But that doesn't answer the longing in our hearts for a relationship with God. But, hiking does show us spiritual truths. And that's the real reason I hike. For every circle made in life, we can learn something that will help us in our spiritual, straight-ahead journey. In the process of completing life's hiking trail, and all the little journeys along the way, we find ways to walk along the Lord's path. From being a little child to having little children of our own, from spending years in school to forgetting all we've learned— everything is circles in our earthly lives except our spiritual journey which leads to our eternal destination.

Thank You, God, for the blessings with journeys in life that will assist me as I press forward in my spiritual walk. I need Your strength for the paths I take in this life. Thank You for the opportunity to hike with You. In Your name I pray, amen.

42

Around the Bend

*As the heavens are higher than the earth,
so are my ways higher than your ways
and my thoughts than your thoughts.*

Isaiah 55:9

Seeing life from near the clouds makes the world seem manageable. Jobs look available. Relationships seem amiable. From the ceiling of the world, the everydayness doesn't get to me. Worry is at an absolute minimum.

One of my favorite things about hiking at high altitudes is the opportunity to look down on a town or a road and watch the people. To objectively see them living their lives brings a new and refreshing perspective on everything. In some ways I can see where they've been and where they will be down the road.

Another aspect of this view is that I can literally see the road beyond where people are at the moment. I glance down and notice the small speck of a car moving down a pencil-thin highway. The road has been clear for miles, and the people on it are traveling at a relaxed, confident speed. But the highway is blocked at a bend in the road by a fallen tree. They can't see it but I can. I could help them find an alternate route around the trouble if they would only look up and follow my directions.

This view of our lives is exactly what God has. He can see the whole of our lives. He thinks beyond the present and sees where we are going. A lifespan is not too long of a stretch for Him to see. He knows where we are on the path of life, and He knows precisely where we need to go.

When I leave the overlooks where I have been peering down on the tiny world I have to go back to, it doesn't take long to return to my limited, human perspective. I can't see where my physical and spiritual trails will ultimately lead. I can't look too far ahead, nor can I see all the dangers that await me along with the detours that will help me skirt them. All I can do is walk and keep my eyes and heart on God, knowing He is watching and waiting to guide me.

Thank You, Father, for Your infinite wisdom. Help me be always willing to listen to You when You speak. It's comforting to know You see the whole of my life—even my journey's end. In Your Son's name I pray, amen.

43

The Surrender

*No one will be able to stand up against you
all the days of your life. As I was with Moses,
so I will be with you; I will never leave you nor forsake you.*

Joshua 1:5

I use an external frame pack. Internal frame packs are all the rage right now, but I prefer the ease of organization with an external frame. Oftentimes, they're cheaper to buy, too.

The design of my pack is simple. There is a frame of metal with padding and shoulder straps that rest on my back. Attached to that frame is a bag with zippers connected to the upper-middle area, which still leaves space above and below for more storage. Internal frame packs are similar, but the frame is *inside* the storage bag, making it difficult to adjust. Internal frames are more streamlined and the pack almost hugs the back. But my external frame has an advantage a manufacturer wouldn't list.

I learned this extra edge from my dad and sister. The trick is this: By raising my hands and reaching behind my head, I can pull the top bar of the frame forward which shifts the weight of the pack off my shoulders. I'm not sure of the physics that make this work, but it is one of my favorite "simple pleasures" on the trail. This little technique works every time.

A revelation hit me one spring morning while on the trail. I had my grip on my pack, relieving my tired shoulders, when I realized how much I looked like someone surrendering. My hands were behind my head and the weight was gone...then it hit me. Surrendering to God takes the burdens away! For a few moments, I had a physical representation of what happens spiritually when I submit and surrender to God.

If you want to buy a fancy internal pack, then be my guest. But if you want to buy a pack that costs less, rides better, is a classic for the hiking community, and shares a spiritual lesson, then go external frame. And remember: *Surrender to God = Burden Lifted.*

As I walk through this life, please remind me that surrendering to You creates lighter loads. Thank You, Jesus, for carrying my burden for me. In Your name I pray, amen.

44

The Strong Foundation

Come, let us rebuild the wall of Jerusalem.

Nehemiah 2:17

My wife and I honeymooned in Charleston, SC, and because Charleston is known as a "walking city," we opted not to rent a car. Stephanie and I love to explore new towns together, and this "hiking trip" offered antique shops, historical sites, and clothing boutiques. We ate at exquisite restaurants where famous chefs prepared delectable dishes. It was truly a wonderful experience.

One morning we decided to leave our "shelter," the King George IV Inn, and head to a nearby historic attraction, Magnolia Plantation. We arranged for a tour company to provide the half-hour van ride, and they picked us up at 8:30 A.M. We greeted our fellow travelers and headed to the grand seventeenth-century plantation spreading along the Ashley River.

Our guide suggested we walk through the gardens before touring the house. This was one of the most beautiful walks I've ever taken! My camera wouldn't quit taking amazing slide photos. Spanish moss hanging in the trees and alligators lounging along the banks of the beautiful ponds were breathtaking. The one-hour day hike was over way too soon.

While the beauty of the surrounding landscape was amazing, there was something more striking that I stumbled upon that morning. It was not something I could capture with my camera, but it became imprinted on my heart.

As our tour guide pointed out, Stephanie and I were standing in a structure that was actually the third version of the plantation house. The Drayton family had moved there in the 1600s, only to have their first house burn down by accident. Later, during the Civil War, the family's second house was burned by Union troops. The third (and present) house was built on the foundation of the second structure using pieces of another home that the Drayton patriarch owned upriver.

The Draytons had determined to make that spot along the Ashley River their home. Their will to bounce back after hardship had overcome the setbacks that repeatedly came. They had built, rebuilt, and built again. I admired their example of faithfulness.

Today's Scripture also tells of a people unwilling to give up. The Jewish people have a history of rebuilding. From the Babylonians to the Nazis, the Israelites have come back to Israel time and time again. One example of this is found in the book of Nehemiah in reference to rebuilding the walls of Jerusalem. Led by Nehemiah, the Israelites were industrious and determined. Eventually they restored on the original foundation the fortified protection that towered around their city. The people were unwilling to let life's circumstances determine where they laughed, worked, and worshiped.

Pondering these two examples of being unwilling to let destruction win, my mind quickly turns to the tragedy of September 11, 2001. As I am writing these words, our troops are in Afghanistan to help them build the peace and freedom that we have known within our borders. Rescue workers are still faithfully cleaning up the wreckage at Ground Zero. We have been hit hard, but we will restore our homeland!

Anything that has any amount of worth will be threatened. We can count on that. But when tough times come, people deal with the loss and move on. Life requires action. Like the Israelites and the Draytons, we must persevere.

We can rebuild a home. We can fill a bank account more than once. We can fight for our freedoms when they've been threatened. We can pray our way back into a life of faith. Sometimes the loss is more personal, such as the death of a relative or a friend. Regardless of the situation, there is hope for restoration in our lives. How? Building on the one and only foundation—Jesus Christ. When we build around Him, our "house" can weather any storm. And not only does Jesus provide a strong foundation, He also provides the strength we need to put everything back together.

> Therefore thus says the Lord GOD, "Behold, I am laying in Zion a stone, a tested stone, a costly cornerstone for the foundation, firmly placed. He who believes in it will not be disturbed" (Isaiah 28:16 NASB).

Lord Jesus, when my life takes an unexpected detour, I turn to You for wisdom and guidance. Help me build a life based on You and Your Word. Amen.

45

Blue Feet

My son, do not despise the LORD's discipline
and do not resent rebuke, because the LORD disciplines
those He loves, as a father the son he delights in.
Proverbs 3:11 – 12

The whole issue of footwear can be tricky. The choices are endless. Sure, you can just grab your sneakers and athletic socks on the way to the trail, but if you encounter rough going or harsh conditions you'll be sorry! The best choice is good boots. First, you need to decide on the style. There are synthetic boots, light-hiker boots, mountaineering boots, and all-leather boots. Second, you have to make the all-important sock decision. These options continue the saga with wool socks, synthetic socks, or cotton socks (they're terrible by the way).

The crux of the issue is avoiding blisters. People are creative in trying to solve this forever problem. Options include double-layered socks, "mole-skin" (a cushioned pad that supposedly reduces blisters), and sock liners. Early in a hiker's career, expect that many different purchases and setups will be auditioned in hopes of finding the perfect method of protecting the last defense between your precious feet and the trail.

Boot, sock, and blister defense all in place, the next step is to hit the trail, find out the setups that do not work, and then settle into a method that functions well. A hiker with less experience, however, will probably forget to think about weathering the rain. Moisture is the worst enemy of footwear. I learned this valuable information quickly, but not early enough.

One of my earliest trips was hiked in a downpour. On this trip I learned how rain and boots and socks become enemies quite quickly. My footwear was brand-new untreated leather, and it lapped up water like thirsty camels. I tried wringing out my socks, but the water just kept flooding in. As a last resort, I created duct-taped, make-shift plastic booties—anything to keep my feet separated from bodies of water. I was having a great hike marred only by some feet trouble.

My route led me past a gas station, and for shelter from the rain I stopped there. While making another adjustment to my miserable feet, something ghastly came into view—my bare feet. They were blue. Totally blue! I was scared to death! I thought, *I'll never walk again. Something is really wrong here.* Then it hit me that my liner socks, one of the many ingredients in my complicated footwear debacle, were navy blue and had never been washed. My feet were only blue from the dye in the material. I was relieved until I looked around.

The patrons of this fine gas-pumping establishment were gawking at me. I'm sure the situation looked terrible. Seeing someone who is visibly drenched from head to toe, obviously a vagabond walking to some distant land, with totally blue feet would create pity, even guilt that humanity could suffer so. What could I have done to be in such peril? They were all perplexed.

What they didn't know is that I was fine. I was having the time of my life! Sure, I was wet, uncomfortable, and fighting my feet, but I was excited to be on the trail. They had no reason to worry.

Have you been in a similar situation? Has your progress on life's path been slow and exhausting, causing others to wonder if you're going to make it? Bear in mind that sometimes hardships are God's way of getting our attention so we can grow spiritually!

When we make mistakes, we, as Christians, get called on the carpet more quickly than unbelievers because God disciplines those He loves. He says, "I love you so much that I'm not going to let you fall away." One of my buddies discovered this in a unique way. Since Danny wondered if the music he listened to displeased God, he went to Him in prayer. He asked whether his choice of music was hindering his spiritual growth. A few days later his radio was stolen from his truck! At first we were horrified. Who could drive without listening to tunes? We thought he'd suffered a terrible blow, but when we asked him about it, we were amazed. Danny was full of joy because God had answered his prayer!

Now maybe your situation is more drastic. But from minor distractions such as blue feet and music to more severe situations such as the loss of a job or a loved one, we can know that God will not give us more than He knows we can handle. First Corinthians 10:13 states: "No temptation has seized you except what is common to man. And God is faithful; he will not let you be tempted beyond what you can bear. But when you are tempted, he will also provide a way out so that you can stand up under it."

When tough times come, we don't need to be embarassed or disheartened. God is leading us, and He cares about our rain-soaked souls!

Jesus, forgive me for sinning against You. Thank You even more for not letting me get away with living contrary to Your Word. I love You, please keep me close to You. In Your name, amen.

46

Light and Wax

You are the light of the world.
A city set on a hill cannot be hidden.
Matthew 5:14

My friend Eric is a master at finding the lightest possible equipment with the least amount of waste. He avoids carrying heavy trash, such as batteries, knowing that a lighter pack provides for quicker feet. A great example of this is his reading light.

I'm not talking about a sophisticated, battery-operated light. Eric's reading light is primitive at best. Even so, it is just the right amount of light for the occasion. His journal and novel continue to grow despite this economical illumination. The design is simple: a small candle with a spring underneath to keep the flame next to the glass housing. It is only about 4 inches tall and weighs around 2 ounces. This "lamp" is the perfect fusion of lightweight design and straight-ahead performance, perfect for his style of hiking. And there's more!

As the candle burns, wax falls to the bottom of this small contraption. The first time I saw the lantern being used, I thought Eric would go through a lot of candles. But Eric had another trick up his sleeve.

The next night, I watched as Eric took pieces of the old wax and placed them near the small flame bravely burning in the harsh weather of high-altitude hiking.

Slowly and patiently, Eric rebuilt the candle by molding and shaping the warm wax until it looked as good as new. I was struck by this procedure. What I thought was used and worthless had become a brand-new light.

Today's Scripture highlights how God can use us to illuminate a dark world with His love. Like the candle, however, we can burn out or the heat of temptation and difficult circumstances may make us melt, leaving a puddle at the bottom of the lamp. Isn't it incredible that although the world may see a dying candle, our heavenly Father takes our lives and reshapes so we can continue to give light to the world.

There is nothing worthless in the kingdom of heaven! No one is so far gone that he or she is tossed in the scrap heap. We may melt, but that makes us more pliable to be molded for God's purposes!

Eric's way of conservation has taught me a lot on the trail. Sometimes reusing gear makes the trip easier to trod. For God, He always finds purpose for what others might consider unusable. He always wishes that we come back to Him, even when we feel all used up.

Lord Jesus, please help me be a light to this dark world. When I start to fall away, please pick me back up and mold me into what You want me to be. Thank You for letting me serve you in so many ways. I praise You today for allowing me to shine for You. In Your name I pray, amen.

47

Deep Freeze Tactics

*If the Spirit of him who raised Jesus from the dead
is living in you, he who raised Christ from the dead
will also give life to your mortal bodies
through his Spirit, who lives in you.*

Romans 8:11

One of the arch enemies on the trail is extreme cold. There's hardly anything more unpleasant than the bitter, stinging wind of a cold front that cuts through clothing and stiffens the toes. While I'm moving I can handle it, but when I stop, I'm a sitting duck. I have nowhere to hide from the intense chill that settles deep inside my body. It feels like the wind ignores my physical presence and pierces right through my ghostlike form on its way to howl in a treetop somewhere down the mountain.

On nights like this, sleeping becomes one of the most challenging feats on the trail. Saving toes and fingers from danger is only one issue. Another is that it's no fun to wake up to a frozen graveyard of gear lying around. Hikers have had to crack into frozen pants, frozen jackets, and rock-hard boots too many times to not figure out ways to save their equipment and bodies from the arctic effect.

For you novice or intermediate hikers out there, here are some techniques for hibernating. Although they won't necessarily keep you nice and cozy in negative degree weather, they will enable you to continue moving down the trail the next morning with minimal difficulty.

Boots, pants, and jackets. The most important gear to save is your boots. The best way to keep these fine works of leather art from becoming big blocks of ice is to use them as a pillow. But don't place them inside your sleeping bag, put the boots *under* it. The heat from your head and shoulder region should be enough to keep frost away. (Sure, the down pillow at home is softer and more relaxing, but the nightmare of walking in stiff, cold boots far outweighs the uncomfortable head rest for the night.) This same idea works for pants and jackets, but tuck them *under the sides* of the sleeping bag. Don't replace your sleeping mat with them entirely, since they could be so wet they might soak through and make your bag very cold and damp.

Water bottles. I broke a great canteen because of not protecting my water bottle through the night. Since dehydration is a danger on the trail, it's good to drink some during the night. But in intensely low temperatures, the water will freeze. The solution? Turn them into teddy bears! Yep! Sleep with your bottles of water. This may seem like a cold idea, but hiker ingenuity has taken care of that, too. Boiling the water before you fill your bottles and slip them into the bag keeps your bottles safe *and* warms your sleeping bag. The water will cool down to drinking temperature in an hour or two.

Human flesh. There's nothing more torturous than being cold throughout the night. When the sun is down and Old Man Winter has you clutched tight, how can you get the all-important Zzzs? The bottles of boiled water help, but the primary starting point is the sleeping bag. There are different ratings for the amount of cold a sleeping bag can perform in. My winter bag is good down to 0 degrees. My spring and fall bag can handle 20 degrees. (I usually keep my 20-degree bag unzipped in June, July, and August.)

If you have the right sleeping bag for the climate, then the key to staying toasty is to wear as few layers as possible inside the bag. Don't pile on the sweaters and jackets and climb inside the zipped-up safe-haven. The extra layers can restrict your blood-flow, which will make you colder. Usually, long underwear and a stocking cap will do. Keep your gloves inside your bag in case your fingers get cold, pull the cord around your face as tightly as you're comfortable with...and drift off to sleep!

These methods for staying warm in a cold climate are great for life in the outdoors, but what can we do when life's wind blows cold? God's plan for staying warm in a frozen world is found in today's verse. Bad news, uncertainty, and disappointment can feel like we're frozen in a cold and dark night. When Jesus lives inside of us, we can maintain our spiritual temperature—even when the cold fingers of this fallen world try to grip our souls. Much like harnessing the heat we naturally give off to keep warm through the night, Jesus keeps our little worlds, our daily lives, from being affected by the bitter cold that wants to penetrate our hearts and minds. Jesus gives us life and protection. He is the key to staying warm through the storms of life.

Jesus, sometimes life turns cold, but I can rest in You and depend upon You to warm my heart and keep me safe. Thank You for being with me through the coldest nights. In Your name I pray, amen.

48

Breaking in New Boots

Saul grew more and more powerful and baffled the Jews living in Damascus by proving that Jesus is the Christ.
Acts 9:22

I needed a new pair of boots. I had been circling a pair at a store in Cleveland, TN, but I was still undecided. During discussions and negotiations with the owner of the hiking supplies store, I was offered the chance to try the boots for a few days by walking up and down my college dorm hallways. As long as I didn't walk outside, I could spend a few hours in the boots, making sure I liked how they felt. The fit was great, so I purchased them... perhaps spending all of my firstborn's college fund.

The boots felt great in the testing stage. I even hiked a few miles before going on a substantial trip to the forest. No matter how hard I had tried, though, I discovered that really breaking them in could only be done during a major hike. I was grateful for my new boots, but they really hurt! My blisters and aches and pains were agonizing signs that I had new leather on my feet. As the trip progressed, my footgear offered as much inconvenience as they did great support and protection. Dealing with this improvement in my hiking gear was going to require major adjustment.

Sometimes the blessings God gives to us require changes in our lives. From a change in careers to different living situations, God may want us to move in a new direction of serving Him. Changes don't easily to most of us.

Saul's life is a great example of this. Before he became an apostle and his name was changed to Paul, he murdered and harassed Christians. After God called him, he was blinded for three days, then God restored his sight. Paul went from persecuting Christians to being a Christian. He moved from a life of living the Law to one of living in grace. He traveled far and wide proclaiming the gospel of Jesus Christ.

Today's verse shows the result of Paul's transformation, but there's more. During his life he went through many hardships because of his faith, including:

> Five times I received from the Jews the forty lashes minus one. Three times I was beaten with rods, once I was stoned, three times I was shipwrecked, I spent a night and a day in the open sea, I have been constantly on the move. I have been in danger from Gentiles; in danger in the city, in danger in the country, in danger at sea; and in danger from false brothers. I have labored and toiled and have often gone without food; I have been cold and naked. Besides everything else, I face daily the pressure of my concern for all the churches (2 Corinthians 11:24-29).

Much like a new pair of boots, a new direction with Jesus or a new blessing He gives might be difficult or feel like an inconvenience for a while. Even though I had trouble with my new boots, I never wanted to go back to hiking in sneakers. No way! I would rather break in new boots than wear old shoes. When God brings blessings our way, we'll be better suited for the journey if we remember that change is sometimes uncomfortable.

Lord Jesus, thank You for bringing blessings my way. Please help me remember that You want the very best for me—even when the change is hard to handle at first. In Your name I pray, amen.

49

How's My Beard?

*We have not ceased to pray for you to ask that
you may be filled with the knowledge of His will...so that
you will walk in a manner worthy of the Lord,
to please Him in all respects, bearing fruit in every
good work and increasing in the knowledge of God.*

Colossians 1:9-10

In the late 1960s and early '70s, a subculture formed and the people involved were referred to as hippies. They showed their liberation from conventional social constructs by not bathing, enjoying nature, keeping their hair long, not shaving, and living simply. Sound familiar? Yep. Maybe inside every hiker a hippie mentality lurks!

Eric and I have had long discussions on the trail concerning the condition of our facial hair. These human bonsai trees grow slowly but surely over a long hike. We don't discuss how *good* they look. No, we like to discuss how *bad* they look. The more rugged and rustic the better. After a few nights on the trail, my beard feels like I could pose for a Civil War Soldier portrait. I imagine long, red locks flowing from my chin down the front of my shirt. How grand it is! I have become a true mountain man! Unfortunately, when Eric and I get back to the truck and glance in the mirror, we discover the reality of thin, scraggly beards that only makes us unkempt. The grizzly look we fantasized didn't measure up to what we saw in our reflections. The "Everest look" once again eludes us.

113

Many Christians have experienced a similar reality check. Sometimes we feel like we have progressed leaps and bounds in our spiritual walk. We weather a couple of trials and assume we have come close to the same trust that Moses had when parting the Red Sea. Maybe a couple of prisons could fall around us like they did for Paul? While being victorious is a good source of encouragement, it's wise to make sure we are realistic about our spiritual growth.

Paul's words in Colossians 1:9-10 reveal the deep desire that more mature saints and our heavenly Father have for our spiritual growth: to "increase in the knowledge of God." Staying on the trail with the Father means growing spiritually, but, like a good beard, it takes time.

James 1:23-24 talks about the person who looks at his reflection then immediately forgets what he looks like. On the trail, it's easy to forget that our beards are still in the infant stage. If we really want that mountain-man look, we need to get back on the trail.

Walking with the Lord includes the lifelong pursuit of deepening our relationship with Him. Hang in there. Eventually, the beard will come.

Lord Jesus, help me grow in You. Thank You for helping me see where I am through Your holy and living Word. Help me always long to draw closer to You. In Your name, amen.

50

Good Stride, Wrong Direction

There is a way that seems right to a man,
but in the end it leads to death.
Proverbs 14:12

The morning was filled with songbirds writing their latest concertos, and the early chill was replaced with a brisk mountain breeze. Eric and I had left a shelter full of sleeping colleagues, and by the time most people were just starting to hike we were passing their shelters at a strong pace. We stopped at one shelter long enough to eat breakfast. The hikers there were doing their normal morning routines. We watched as sleeping bags were crammed back into their stuff sacks and extra water was poured onto the ground, forming little patches of mud around the shelter door. The *zzzzip* of packs finally ready to go occurred between jokes and goodbyes.

As one hiker was leaving, he stopped to ask where Eric and I were from. Our short conversation revealed the nondescriptive details people give to strangers. The conversation ended well, and the stranger gave a "hiker dude" blessing to the remainder of our trip. When he turned to walk away, though, he made a miscalculation.

Instead of swinging around to head down the trail, the man started trekking down the well-worn path to the designated "restroom" area. Eric and I let out a big laugh while his buddy yelled to get his attention. The hiker seemed rather embarrassed, but genuine moments of laughter are relished, so the rest of us hikers probably laughed a little longer than necessary. We'd all been there, done that.

As Christians, we can think we're heading the right way. We're bold in our stride, making good time—down the wrong trail! Even if we look like we know what we are doing, it's still the wrong direction.

Isn't it a blessing that God gives us good friends who will get our attention and direct us back to the right path? Even if we get embarrassed for the moment, it is better than walking into the spiritual wilderness!

So let's not be so confident that we don't watch where we're going. We need to keep our ears open for those people in our lives who may help us stay on track. We can be confident that the Lord will always direct us, but part of being led is not being afraid to hear, "Wrong way, the path is over here." And don't be afraid to reach out and help someone else who is lost.

Lord, You know the way I should go much better than I. Please guide me in the right direction and help me stay on Your path. Thank You, Lord Jesus, amen.

51
Camping vs. Hiking

"Come, follow me," Jesus said.
Matthew 4:19

Soon after Stephanie and I met, the issue of hiking came up. I told her that I love to traipse off into the woods in pursuit of memories, spectacular views, and the physical challenge of racking up the miles. Even though she had never hiked before, she said it sounded like fun. I was delighted by her positive response! We started to talk about how great it would be to go with a group on a backpacking trip. I then asked her how she envisioned hiking.

She told me that she could cook dinner in a black kettle—beef stew with carrots and potatoes. Over the open fire, she would make cornbread or biscuits, and then dessert would be cookies and coffee, which she would make with a percolator on the open flame. The next day, after a pancake breakfast, we would hike or "whatever," and then camp next to a stream where we could catch fish and fry them over another campfire. Then we could go home and get cozy, make some hot chocolate, and talk about our trip.

I was completely floored by her version of hiking. Backpacking trips are nothing like that. I've hiked a lot, but I've never had a trip like that!

I told Stephanie that with her vision, a car would have to be about 30 yards away, especially since black kettles are heavy! Furthermore, I seldom light a fire on the trail. Sometimes it's nice, but packing food that requires the use of campfires isn't wise because sometimes the weather doesn't cooperate. My objections went on and on until I finally realized Stephanie and I were discussing two different activities. Backpacking and camping are not the same.

Now, for those who are thinking, "Stephanie's version of being outdoors sounds a lot better," I can see your point. But when the goal is to carry a light pack, log lots of miles, and leave the comforts of home to truly experience God's great outdoors, camping just doesn't cut it.

The main difference between backpacking and camping is summed up in this question: "Where's your car?" Campers usually have a car close by. It's their getaway vehicle if times get rough; it's their shelter in the rain; it's their heater if the night turns cold.

As Christians, sometimes this confusion between camping and backpacking finds its way into our walk with the Lord. When Jesus approached the men chosen to be His disciples, He asked them to follow Him. Even though they had grown up with religion and it was their way of life, religion had never asked them to leave their comfort zones. The Law never made them walk away from who they were—and that was the big difference. Jesus asked them to *leave everything*.

Matthew 4:20 reads, "At once they left their nets and followed him." The men walked away from all they had depended on. They were stepping into a whole new world that relied solely on Jesus. Isn't that an exciting and amazing choice to make?

Spiritually some of us are still camping. We go through the motions of living in the forest of religion. Some folks believe they are doing all that is needed to stay on the straight and narrow path. But how close is the car? How much distance has actually been covered?

Religion *is not* Christianity. Religion might have some resemblance to following Jesus (prayer, fasting, worship), but it doesn't scratch the surface of true Christianity. Instead of camping through this life with Jesus, we are called to "huff it" down the path He has put beneath our feet. As the writer of Hebrews tells us, "Let us run with perseverance the race marked out for us." If our eyes are fixed on Jesus and His glory, the old car at the beginning of the trail will be a ridiculous alternative to the amazing adventures the real trail holds.

Lord Jesus, take away my fears. Give me the strength to walk away from "religion"—to leave it all behind and follow You. Thank You for asking me to join You on the path of righteousness. I love You and respond wholeheartedly to Your call. In Your name I pray, amen.

52

When We Have to Be Away

I have hidden your word in my heart
that I might not sin against you.
Psalm 119:11

Soon after the tragic events on September 11, 2001, I longed to head to the forest with my pack and hike until my legs would take me no farther. I needed the canopy of the trees and clouds to allow my heart time to cope and heal. The soothing spring water and the magnificent sunsets were just what I needed. But I couldn't go.

I had just started a new job, and Stephanie and I were planning a wedding that would take place in a few weeks. If ever the time was not right for hiking, it was the weeks after the tragedy. Maybe some of you also wanted to hit the trail while coming to terms with with one of our nation's darkest days. It would have been the perfect time and way to escape.

During that tragic time, I found a way to get to the trail without ever leaving home—I wrote a song. The centerpiece of the lyric is what being on the hiking trail does for a hiker's soul:

Tennessee Hills

My mother was raised in the country
She worked hard while the morning was black

And my father was raised in the city
But once he found those hills his heart never came
   back
And sometimes I find myself up early in the morning
Just to work my fingers down to any old bone
And sometimes I find myself heading to the hills
Those Tennessee hills that let me be all alone
Oh, those Tennessee hills that let me be all alone

I've seen smoke upon a horizon
In a city far away from my home
But not so far if you measure the distance
From my eyes and my ears to the center of my soul
And sometimes I find myself up early in the morning
Just to work my fingers down to any old bone
And sometimes I find myself heading to the hills
Those Tennessee hills that let me be all alone
Oh, those Tennessee hills that let me be all alone

I'm sure you can especially relate to the phrase, "Those Tennessee hills that let me be all alone." We have memories of being on the trail that are so vivid that, even when we can't get there, we still found solace thinking or writing about it.

One thing that I did find comforting was entering the doors of our church here in Nashville and reading scripture, singing songs, and praying with other Christians. Those days of mourning and outrage bonded us all close together. How grateful we all were to have each other, even as we grieved for the families who had lost their courageous loved ones.

We can't always make it to a church when we are hurting. Sometimes bad things happen and we are away from our copy of the Good Book. What do we do when life keeps us away from what helps us heal? That's where today's scripture comes in.

Like I mentioned earlier, I have memorized all the wonderful things about being on the trail. At a moment's notice I can feel the weight of my pack shift as I take one more strong step up an incline dauntingly poised above. The birds are chirping and singing. Later, the heat rises as I cook dinner on my little stove. The feel of my leather boots after a long day, the view from a high ridgeline, a beautiful sunrise, hot coffee, and a delicious serving of oatmeal satisfies all my senses.

Hiding God's Word in our hearts makes it readily available at all times. We can call up all the wonderful promises of peace and assurance He gives to carry us through tough times. We can hear His voice speak truth to our troubled souls. We can dwell on the grand view of how wide and deep His love is for us. If we are faithful to walk the paths of Scripture daily, we take with us on the trail of life the knowledge and power that heals our broken hearts and soothes our souls.

Heavenly Father, thank You for Your Word. Help me memorize it so that troubled times don't leave me stranded in despair. Thank You for speaking to my heart each day. In Your name I pray, amen.

53

Two Shadows

Two are better than one, because they have a good return
for their work: If one falls down, his friend can help him up.
But pity the man who falls and has no one to help him up!

Ecclesiastes 4:9-10

Soon after our honeymoon, Stephanie and I decided to go for an afternoon hike. We chose a nearby nature trail that meanders through the woods surrounding a beautiful body of water called Radnor Lake. The day was perfectly cool and sunny, and we were looking forward to the one hour trek in the hills.

After only a short distance on the path, I noticed something completely foreign to my previous hiking experiences. There were two shadows side by side! I have hiked with other people before, but no matter how big the group, I always walked alone, with others close behind or in front of me. I had never hiked arm in arm with another person.

As you know, hiking can be hard work. It's not something that one can do well in close proximity to another person. There are legs pumping, feet kicking up dust, elbows flailing, and eyes looking for dramatic views. It's not easy to hold someone close during this invigorating activity. Suddenly, I realized that this situation echoes marriage. Walking through this life is no piece of cake. It might seem like walking alone, not needing someone else, would be easier. In hard times when a lot of work has to be done to survive, coordinating with someone else can be frustrating. There are plenty of opportunities for a wayward elbow to accidentally crack someone in the head.

Our verse in Ecclesiastes shows the beauty of trekking through life with a companion. If you get injured on the trail, someone is there to help you. Bad situations can often be solved quickly when someone gives a helping hand. Does this mean you're up a creek if you're single? Absolutely not! Hiking with friends and family offers similar help and comfort. Whomever you choose to walk with in this life, be it spouse, friends, or relatives, make sure that Jesus is your primary companion.

The perfect companion on the trail of life, Jesus not only holds us close, but He knows the way and never makes mistakes. We can be tough and independent on the trail; we can be rugged and capable in the mountains. But no matter how strong and knowledgeable we are, we can't make it alone.

Thank You, Lord, for being my companion on the trail. Help me walk with others the same way You walk with me. I love You. In Jesus' name, amen.

54

Heading Home

*But while he was still a long way off, his father
saw him and was filled with compassion for him.*

Luke 15:20

It's the last day of your hike. A week, a month, maybe more has gone by since you've seen your family and friends. You miss their laughter and smiles. You miss the people who know you and the people you trust. The camping meals that were so fun to eat at first are tasting like boiled cardboard and cheap flavoring.

Imagine a nice steak. No, don't imagine it…it makes life on the trail too hard. With a baked potato. Mmmm. Hot, freshly baked rolls dripping with butter. Too much? Then don't think of a hot fudge sundae. And, at the end of a long day hiking, a hot shower…soap…shaving, deodorant. No, don't think about it. You might get frustrated and homesick.

These are the things we leave behind as mundane and return to as glorious perks. There's something about going home to everything you know that feels wonderful and right. Hiking and camping are fun, but what would a journey be without a journey's end?

In the Bible, there is a story of a young man who finds a glorious end to a difficult journey. Perhaps you are familiar with the parable of the prodigal son. The son, who has gone away to live life as he pleases, returns to his father, his family, and his father's table to enjoy the things he left behind for youthful ambitions. After squandering his inheritance, he feels great joy when he realizes his father still accepts him. When we get to heaven, there will also be family, friends, and other believers waiting for us. We will be with those we know and love and trust. And just like we need to clean up after the journey on the trail makes us dirty, stinky, and less than presentable, God is going to give us new clothes and new bodies that do not ache with the ups and downs we endure in this world.

We trek through the forest with our goal in mind. Like the prodigal son's final miles of his hike back home, we know there is something awesome that awaits us. And in that same way, as we move through this world, there is something astounding ahead. This journey does have an end—spending time with Jesus in heaven!

The difference going from forest to home is amazing. The cozy glow of a lamp and a refreshing, warm shower make us realize that life in the civilized world is not so bad. But imagine the difference when we reach our heavenly home! No pain. No suffering. I'm sure the food is beyond belief. And our family and friends who've chosen Jesus will be there. The best part will be when our Father takes us in His arms and says, "Welcome home."

While this is where we live, learn, and love, it is only for a moment. The ultimate goal in our journey with God cannot be found on earth's terrain. The Earth is beautiful, but it's not our final home. Whether we are camping in the forest or living in the suburbs, all earthly homes are temporary tents. And whether we walk with companions or strike out on our own, we are never alone. For those of us who love our Creator, we can always know that no matter where we walk, we are hiking with God.

Thank You, Jesus, for the hope of the journey's end. In Your name I pray, amen.

The Outdoor Pocket Book Series

Reel Time with God

With God on a Deer Hunt

With God on the Hiking Trail

With God on the Open Road